Introduction to the Real World

101 Tips for Real World Freshmen

Written by

KAZ NAGAI

Copyright © 2019 by Kaz Nagai

All rights reserved. No part of this book may be reproduced or used in any manner without written permission of the copyright owner except for the use of quotations in a book review. For more information, address:

First paperback edition May 2019

Edited by Nathan Foreman
Book design by Alex Pooler

ISBN 978-1-7331135-0-2 (paperback)

Dedicated to all my students.

Table of Contents

INTRODUCTION

CHAPTER 1: WORK

1. The Real World is Way Better than College!
2. What if Your First Job Sucks?
3. 5 People You want to be Friends with at Work
4. Build the Mindset to Lead People, not Manage them
5. Build a Quick and Solid Foundation of Trust By Offering Your Help
6. Have an Entrepreneurial Mind Set
7. Use S.L.A.C.K.E.R When You Receive Criticism
8. Ask Questions
9. Use the 5 Whys Technique
10. Pack Your Own Lunch
11. Don't Eat Lunch Alone!
12. See Your Job at a Macro Level rather than a Micro Level
13. Map out an Organizational Chart
14. Spend One Long Day in Your First Month at the Office
15. Network, Network, Network!
16. Think like an Employer rather than an Employee.
17. Early Bird Gets the Worm
18. Don't Multi-task but Learn How to Deal with Multiple Tasks
19. Have an Exit Strategy
20. Leave or Not Leave?

CHAPTER 2: RELATIONSHIP/SOCIAL

21. Unwind and Live Simple
22. Slow and Steady Wins the Race... Very Rarely
23. Say Goodbye to Social Anxiety
24. Meet People
25. Reconnect with Your Old Network
26. Social Media can Ruin Your Job
27. We are Addicted to Cell Phones and Social Media
28. Invisible Wall
29. Communication is the Foundation of Building Good Relationships.
30. Men Love Their Man Cave; Women Love Their Girl Friends
31. Give What the Other Person Wants, not What You Want the Other Person to Have
32. Emotional Needs
33. Make Your Good Habits Your Routines!
34. Create a Mini-traditions
35. Road Trips
36. Bucket List
37. North Star
38. Strategic Meeting
39. The Art of Asking for Help from Your Partner
40. Relationships Require Continuous Education from Both Ends

41. Female Brain vs Male Brain
42. Three Types of Empathy

CHAPTER 3: HAPPINESS
43. Misconceptions
44. Our Minds Lie to Us about What Will Make Us Happy
45. Science of Happiness
46. Make Time for Social Connections
47. Good and Bad on Social Media
48. Help Others
49. Give Gratitude
50. E.S.M – Exercise, Sleep, Meditate
51. Be in the Moment
52. Invest in Time
53. Love won't Make You Happy
54. To Be or Not to Be (Married)
55. Flow
56. Awe
57. Accept
58. Too Many Options Make People Miserable
59. Synthetic Happiness

CHAPTER 4: FINANCE
60. Richest Time of Your Life
61. Financial Rules of Thumb
62. Take Advantage of Tax Benefits and Have Multiple Financial Options.
63. Financial Tips
64. Don't Save Money
65. Investments
66. Open Multiple Checking Accounts
67. Monthly Expenses Account
68. Pros and Cons on Credit Cards
69. HELOC
70. Life Insurance

CHAPTER 5: COMMUNICATION
71. It's You
72. Communication Style
73. Listen Actively
74. A Good Communication Fulfills a Women's Primary Love Need
75. How to Persuade Others
76. Humor
77. Talk to Strangers
78. Rock-Paper-Scissors: 100% Winning Strategy
79. Body Language

CHAPTER 6: SELF-IMPROVEMENT
80. Stay Positive
81. Time Budgeting
82. How Should You Spend Time in Your 20s?

83. Love Yourself
84. Unlock Black Boxes
85. Problem-Solving Scenarios
86. Note Taking
87. Start Something
88. To Be or Not to Be (Stressed)
89. Friend or Foe
90. Labeling Creates an Environment
91. Success
92. Leadership
93. Decision Making
94. Speak at a High Level of Consciousness
95. Tips for Parents
96. Every Day Should Have a Nap
97. Take a Detour in Your Life
98. Want to vs Can
99. Follow Your Passion While Living out Your Purpose
100. Turn Your Worst Nightmare into Your Assets
101. Sugar Lies

CONCLUSION
APPENDIX
ABOUT THE AUTHOR

INTRODUCTION

LETTER TO THE READER

It didn't hit me untill the day after my college graduation. I said to myself, "Well, I just graduated from college. Now what?" I had a degree in math, but sadly, I didn't know what to do with that. I had zero plans for my life, not having applied to a single job prior to my graduation. I also had no internships or experiences besides coaching kids' baseball. Yes, I know. I should've thought about my future a little bit more seriously. But my extreme Type B personality made me think everything was going to be ok.

I was scared not knowing what would happen next, but at the same time I was excited because I had nothing but options. I decided that I should try 10 new things a year for the next five or six years because I knew this was the best time to do so. I learned Spanish, backpacked for two months, traveled the world, coached in a collegiate summer baseball league, taught in school, consulted international teams in the U.S. and Europe, learned how to dance salsa, and many other things. One pursuit led me to another, and before I knew it, there were opportunities everywhere.

If you're about to graduate or have recently graduated from a college or high school, and you're entering the Real World, I know how you feel. It's both scary and exciting, isn't it? First – remember that everything is going to be okay. It always will be. But how you spend the next five years will impact your life the most. I can say confidently that the next five years are more important than your previous 16 years in school. That's not just my personal opinion; the majority of people I talked to while writing this book said the same thing.

I asked many people what advice they would give to new grads. I also collected data using surveys through my website. This book is a collection of my experiences and other people's voices. There isn't a one-size-fits-all solution to life, but I hope you find something useful in this book. Enjoy it, but most of all, enjoy your life, because you live only once!

Very truly,
Kaz Nagai

CHAPTER 1: WORK

Most likely, your work is the biggest source of excitement for you right now. At the same time, it is also likely your biggest source of fear. Although you might have had part-time jobs while in school, a Full-time job is a totally different animal because you will be spending at least a third of your life from now on in the office. Another third is to sleep, and the remaining time is for whatever.

Can you imagine spending a third of your life in a miserable working environment?

It can happen to anyone. It surely happened to me. My first few years in the real world was the most stressful time of my life. I was grumpy all the time because of how I spent my time at work.

Then I realized that I was letting the environment control me. I should be controlling the environment instead.

This section of the book would've helped me go through the toughest time of my life if I had read it. Obviously, it's too late for me but I hope it's not too late for you.

1. The Real World is Way Better than College!

In spite of its challenges, I still believe that the Real World is better than college. You meet new people, learn new knowledge, and explore new cities if you move for work. It sounds like your freshman year in college, doesn't it? That's why you are a Real-World Freshman now. This time, however, is much better.

The biggest change you'll feel is that you are given so many more options. What you decide matters a lot more than before. You'll have a lot more money, too. In fact, you have more money now than the next 20 years (I'll cover that in Finance section). It doesn't mean you should be going to Starbucks every day though.

Being in school was easy. Everything was structured. You showed up at a certain location at a certain time. For the Real World, things are less structured. You'll have to be flexible at work depending what it requires you to do. The outcome, though, will be much more meaningful to you. For example,

The project you spent a month to complete in school might have given you a grade of A, but the project you spend a month to complete in the real world might change someone's life.

Just like in sports, there are a pre-season, a regular season, and a post-season. You just finished your pre-season in Life. In the next however many years before you retire, you will be in Life's regular season. Make it count because not everyone gets to the post-season.

2. What if Your First Job Sucks?

Danny, a friend of mine, always said this to people. In fact, this comes from his experience. He applied for the job of his dream but didn't get it. However, the company did offer him another job that he ended up taking as his first full time job. His working hours were brutal. Nights and weekends meant nothing to him.

One of many things about him that I admired was that he had the mentality of "**What doesn't kill you makes you stronger**".

He stayed in the same position for a while, giving his best effort till another opportunity came up. He wouldn't have had any chance getting the new opportunity without the experience from the first job.

Your first job might not be the one you wanted. In fact, you might not enjoy it at all. But do your best at it - it might lead you to a new opportunity.

It doesn't take a long time to find out whether you like the job or not. But it does take a long time to build your relationships and networks with people. That's your priceless asset that you don't want to take for granted. I am a big believer of this saying, **it's not whom you know but it's who knows you that matters the most** (I'll cover that more thoroughly in the Relationship section). That was exactly what Danny was doing in this first job - building relationships and networks within the company in his first job. The hiring manager for his next opportunity had worked with Danny before and believed he was the best fit for the position.

His attitude towards his job and his networking made it happen.

That being said, it's a different story if your job is not healthy for you at all. To leave the company is an option if that's the case, (more details later in this section). Consult with your mentor (if you have one) or someone close. That is why the next topic is important. It's about whom to befriend at work.

3. 5 People You Want to be Friends with at Work

Most likely you will spend a third of every day with the people at work. It's not too much to say that they will make your days or ruin them. Additionally, you do not just become friends with them. You also support and take care of one another. Here is the top 5 people you should be friends with.

1. **Receptionist**: Your days will start off by seeing the receptionist. It might as well start off with a big smile!!

2. **Cleaning Services**: They take care of you. You take care of them by stopping your work and talking to them, offering them a chocolate (who wouldn't like chocolates??), and sending them a thank you note once in a while. Yes, I understand that it's their job to clean. But if you were they, whom would you rather cleanup for, a nice person or a complete jerk? I remember my cleaning friends actually cried when I told them I was leaving my previous company.

3. **Your IT go-to person**: After you restart your computer three times and it still has problems, it's time to call your personal IT friend. Truth is that they can come fix your computer much faster than the traditional way, which is you calling your company IT Help desk. Buy them a cup of coffee on Monday because many problems seem to happen on Monday.

4. **Happy Hour Coordinator**: Need I say more?

5. **Mentor:** It's nice to have someone to talk about your future with. You make fewer mistakes and get where you want to be quicker with their guidance. If your company doesn't have a mentoring program, find someone who has your dream position or job and ask them to be your mentor. Most likely the person will help you out.

I personally like to add baristas who can make a cup of coffee with an amazing design on top to the list. For some reason they are always happy and nice, which makes my day when I visit them. Unfortunately, they didn't make it into the top 5, since not all companies have coffee shops on their campus (usually there are coffee machines in the lounge). If your company hires their own barista, lucky you!!

4. Build the Mindset to Lead People, not Manage Them

Effective leaders encourage others to achieve their personal goals and contribute to their teams for the accomplishment of their objectives. Leaders are often considered to be Role Models for others to emulate. They provide guidance and feedback throughout the course of assigned projects and often help others improve their skills.

You can be both a leader and a manager at the same time. But make sure that you know the difference. The objects and methods of Leading and Managing are different. Leading deals with people, whether they are individuals or groups. Great leaders inspire others to follow them. Managing deals mostly with things, like planning, organizing, and facilitating specific tasks.

Work done by those who are Lead is more productive and thorough than work done by those who are merely told what to do. Their motivation level is very different.

So, how do you lead people? Simon Sinek, one of the most famous TED Talk speakers, puts it beautifully.

They (Leaders) are supposed to be caring for us and helping us realize our own value. If you have anybody who reports to you, your responsibility is not to make them meet the deadline. Your responsibility is not to make sure that they do as you say. Your responsibility is to make sure they understand their own strengths, their own value, and that they are way more talented than they think they are. The only way they'll learn that is if you put them in situations in which they fail and you hold them and you support them and you give them talent and you give them skills and you give them education and you watch their backs. If they fall over, you encourage them to get back up. If they fall over, you encourage them to get back up. If they fall over, you encourage them to get back up until they figure it out themselves.

Leadership contains some of the following characteristics (non-exhaustive)

- Authoritative
- Affiliative
- Coaching/Mentoring
- Democratic
- Altruistic
- Innovative

I've been blessed with leaders who were very supportive and understanding throughout my career. But some people may not be that lucky. The truth is though, that you can learn no matter what kind of leaders you have. If you have really good ones, copy what they do. If you have really bad ones, don't be like them because you know how people the people you may lead will feel if you act like them.

5. Build a Quick and Solid Foundation of Trust By Offering Your Help

Just because you are a newbie, doesn't mean you **only receive** help from others. **You** can help others, too. Especially when someone needs to leave early or is running out of time, a simple offer of help will sound like music to their ears.

This kind of behavior is a win-win situation for a newbie. You, as a newbie, get to learn something new. Your co-worker gets jobs done quicker. It also builds trust and reliability between you. The next thing you know, word will spread, and new doors will open for you.

However, it gives a different perspective if your co-worker asks for help rather than you are offering. That's basically just assigning work to a newbie. There is nothing special about that. There is nothing special about experienced workers helping other experienced workers, either.

What's special is when you offer help as a newbie, which says a lot about you.

Building trust and reliability among co-workers takes time. It doesn't get done overnight. Fortunately, you can take a shortcut and do that as a newbie. You may not see such opportunities but trust me - they are everywhere. Your managers and co-workers would love to hear you say you want to help. It doesn't have to be every day. Offering a help once every week or two will take you to a new level of trust in their minds.

6. Have an Entrepreneurial Mindset

Your first job might be tedious and technical, but it doesn't mean you have to do only what you are told to do. If you think your lower-level position only contains passive tasks, then you might want to think twice because there is a lot more you can put on the table than just what you are told to do.

You are unique and special because your life experience is different from anyone else in the office. You might have done or seen things in the past that might be applicable to the company. If so, then you need to speak up and present your ideas.

This is a good opportunity to find out whether your voice is heard or not by your company. If the company ignores the voices of their employees at any level or position, then I highly recommend you leave the company. Otherwise, your stress level will keep rising throughout your career.

Find out whether your company respects the employees' voices, not only top-level people's voices.

For example, a friend of mine was in an IT position. He believed that getting all the employees together in one place once a year to celebrate the company's success was a good way to appreciate the jobs and the company. Although his position had nothing to do with the company's workplace improvement, his idea was brought up and presented in the board meeting. Now the company has an Annual All Employee Meeting.

If you believe in one thing that helps the company, make sure you speak up about it. Your managers knowing that you are trying to help the company is always a good thing. It's cool that you never know what kind impact your ideas can make till it becomes reality. Keep thinking like an Entrepreneur.

7. Use S.L.A.C.K.E.R When You Receive Criticism

Do you have trouble accepting criticism? If so, I have a solution for you.

I was one of those people who had a tough time hearing negative feedback. In fact, I used to get offended and angry easily. I knew I had to change my attitudes but didn't know how. After many trials and errors, I created a useful tool called S.L.A.C.K.E.R.

NO, I'm not talking about a slacker as a lazy person. S.L.A.C.K.E.R is an acronym of 7 recommended actions against negative feedback. They are

Stay Positive
Listen Actively
Ask Questions
Complement the Feedback
Keep Improving yourself
Earn Trust Back
Remember to Say Thank You

Here is an example. I like to speak in public. I videotaped myself in one of my speeches and showed it to my wife. She watched the clip and said "You looked like a used car salesman. A really bad one."

I couldn't believe what I heard because I was confident about my speech. She also gave me more feedback afterwards, 19 negative and 1 positive, to be precise. The only one positive was that she liked the end of my speech where I walked off the stage…

Then I applied S.L.A.C.K.E.R. I stayed positive about her comments because she didn't mean to hurt my feeling, but she wanted me to become a better speaker. I listened actively to what she meant rather than what she said. I asked her questions to confirm whether what I thought she meant was correct. I complemented her feedback because all of her points were correct. I kept improving myself by applying her feedback to my next speech. I earned her trust back because she enjoyed my next speech much more. In the end, I remembered to thank her.

Here is another way to look at this.

If nobody says anything to you anymore, it's because they've given up on you.

S.L.A.C.K.E.R. is a good reminder to take corrective actions when your not meeting others' expectations. Use S.L.A.C.K.E.R. When you receive criticism and your personal growth will be guaranteed.

8. Ask Questions

This is the best time for you to absorb knowledge and information easily, like a sponge. The fact that you are new to the position allows you to ask any kind of question. That's right. There are no dumb questions. I understand that you want to figure things out on your own and impress your managers. But it's actually better that you ask questions and not try to reinvent the wheel. There are procedures because someone has already spent some time to establish them. Your managers expect you to figure things out by yourself later on your career, not now.

Here are two quick reminders:
1. Use Open-Ended questions.
2. If you don't know, say you don't know.

Another thing about questions is that the type of question matters. At first, you might be asking many technical questions, which is expected. As you gain knowledge, you should be asking more theoretical questions rather than technical. It's a lot easier to offer improvements if you understand the issues theoretically.

There will be a time when someone else will ask you questions about things you are doing. You should be able to answer questions at a theoretical level rather than just a technical level by then.

If I were given an hour in which to do a problem upon which my life depended, I would spend the first 55 minutes determining the proper question to ask, for once I know the proper question, I could solve the problem in less than five minutes. – Albert Einstein

This was one of the common answers from a survey I conducted. According to the survey, newly graduated young people do not ask enough questions. It's as if they were supposed to figure things out by themselves. The truth is that Managers and co-workers would like to hear you ask many questions. You should challenge them by asking hard questions, which gives you (and them) an opportunity to learn deeply about a certain subject or something new.

Just be sure not to ask the same questions over and over. Ask proper questions and takes notes!

9. Use the "5 Whys" Technique

Toyota Motor Corporation, one of the largest vehicle companies in the world, developed a technique as a critical component of its problem-solving training. It was back in 1950s when the people in the Toyota Production System started using the technique by repeating why five times to investigate the nature of the problem as well as the solutions. This technique allows you to dig into each problem until the root-cause is found.

This technique is used in many different industries now as a part of their problem-solving approach.

Here is an example. The Stone exterior was deteriorating at the Jefferson Memorial in Washington DC. Repairing the stone or painting over the worn areas was too expensive. Then they asked 5 whys.

1) Why was the stone deteriorating? -> Because high-powered sprayers are used often to wash the memorial
2) Why are the high-powered washings used often? -> Because of so many bird droppings
3) Why are there so many birds? -> Because they come to feed on spiders
4) Why are there so many spiders? -> Because they feed on insects at night
5) Why are there so many insects at night? Because they are attracted by lights that shine on the memorial at night

The root-cause here was the insects attracted by the lights. Once they found it out, they reduced the amount of time the memorial spent in the spotlight. They saved money from not only the electricity bills but also from the fact they didn't need to hire the high-powered sprayers anymore.

I've mentioned that this technique was used in many industries. A nice thing about the technique is that you can use it in your relationship, too.

Here is another example. My wife and I were going through many ups and downs like a roller-coaster when we had our first child. It seemed like our marriage was going downhill. We tried the 5 whys...

1) Why is our marriage at risk? -> Because it's stressful.
2) Why is it stressful? -> Because we argue often.
3) Why do we argue often? -> Because we communicate poorly.
4) Why do we communicate poorly? -> Because we don't sit down face to face to talk.
5) Why do we not sit down face to face? -> Because we don't have any time for each other.

We realized that what we needed to do was to spend some quality time together. Once we did that, we communicated more effectively, and didn't argue as often. Then our marriage became less stressful.

What if we asked only one why? "Marriage was stressful -> get massage". It probably wouldn't save our marriage, would it?

10. Pack Your Own Lunch

It doesn't matter whether you are single living by yourself, or don't cook at home, because packing your own lunch serves two purposes. First, it's a lot cheaper to bring your own lunch than buying it at a restaurant or café. Depending on the city where you live, the average lunch can go from $8 ~ $15 plus tips multiplied by 20 working days in a month, which can go up to $300+/month. That can go towards your car payment if you pack your own lunch!

Second, it's easier to make your life healthier because you can control when and what to eat. It takes a few minutes in the morning to pack a few snacks, fruits and last night's left overs. This allows you to eat small portions throughout the day rather than a big meal at lunch time. One of the benefits of eating small portions is keeping your blood sugar level within an ideal range, which keeps your metabolism high and keeps you away from diabetes. Another benefit is helping you maintain steady energy levels and a balanced appetite throughout the day.

It's time to say goodbye to those Maruchan Cup Ramen Noodles that you used to eat for lunch in college, even though they are cheap and quick! Your body needs more nutritious foods than cup noodles.

Additionally, this is the best time to learn how to cook if you haven't already. And it's the best time to increase the number of recipes in your head (or in your bookshelf). This is a must-have skill as you will have to serve your family one day. You might be already a master of the grill from all the tailgate experiences at college, but your family needs to eat something other than burgers, right?

Become a decent chef for your family. You don't have to be like a professional. But having efficient skills in the kitchen will save you when you have to serve for your family, because you can't spend two hours each day after work trying to learn how to cook for them while you make dinner.

So learn how to cook today. Pack the left overs for lunch tomorrow. Then save $ and stay healthy

By the way, if you know how to cook, that is a huge plus in a relationship!

11. Don't Eat Lunch Alone!

You are now at the steepest part of the learning curve, yet the learning doesn't occur only in the office.

Lunch time is one of the best times to learn something else rather than your tasks at your office.

For example, going out lunch with someone from a different department will help you to connect the dots of how your job impacts other departments. Going out to lunch with someone who has been there for a long time will help you map an organizational chart within the company.

A TV News host said once in his show, that he spent almost 2 hours every day, eating lunch with different persons each day, for networking and self-improvement. That helped him get his current position. He mentioned that he used the opportunity to expand his knowledge and experience other people's point of views, which allowed him to stay neutral on every subject his news show covered.

Sure, not all of us can take 2 hours for lunch every day. But eating with other people for even 30 minutes will refresh your brain and recharge you. It's so much better than eating lunch at your desk. Splitting a day into multiple segments makes you more efficient, productive, and creative throughout your day.

Here is the reason. The thinking part of the brain called the Prefrontal Cortex keeps you focused on your goals when you work. But it does more than just that. It is also responsible for planning complex cognitive behavior, logical thinking, executive functioning, personality expression, modeling social behavior, and much more. It's no wonder why it needs a few breaks!

The truth is that your office is full of interesting, intelligent, and amazing people. Get to know them and ask them questions. Plus, foods taste better when you have a companion, right??

12. See Your Job at a Macro Level rather than a Micro Level

Your first job might be a series of tedious tasks such as mailing envelopes, making copies, or ordering caterers for lunch meetings. Some days may make you feel empty and underappreciated. You may even feel like you have not accomplished anything or contributed to the company.

No worries. You need to look at things as a big picture, at a Macro level, since seemingly insignificant tasks can create a huge amount of value for your organization, whether you see it or not. The envelopes you mail will bring potential customers in to the business. The Information packages you create will make the business transactions easier and smoother. The potential customers enjoy the presentation in a nice lunch meeting with the food you order. When everything goes well, you are a big part of success.

**ered*Tedious tasks are tremendously meaningful. Every little thing matters.*

If it's still hard to see the full impact of your work for the company, remember - every little part of a car, such as a gear, tire, or bolt, is necessary for the car to run.

Also, in case you want to start your own business in the future, you must be able to see things at the macro level and know it all. A friend of mine started as a field technician for an energy company. He did it all from fixing electrical stuff to managing people and cash flow. Later on, he started own energy company. He did have up and downs in the business like any others. His experience at his first company, looking at every little thing in a big picture, helped him to achieve his goal.

Another reason you want to look at your position and your tasks at a macro level is to see whom your work impacts. The next topic will explain the benefits of knowing the other people at work

13. Map Out an Organizational Chart

Within the first few weeks working for your company, your manager may give you the chart, or go over the organizational relationships between employees. If they have a chart, that's very helpful. Otherwise, spend some time talking to managers and co-workers to map out the relationships within the organization, and make your own chart. This is another way to look at the company as a big picture.

It's easy to get caught up in your own circle and not to go outside of that. It's easy to get comfortable when you see your own work affecting only those within the circle. The truth is that what you do goes beyond that circle and affects many people even outside of your department.

Knowing all the people that your work affects is a two-way benefit. In one project you may be working for people outside the circle. They will work with you, treat you, and thank you differently if they know you compared to if they don't know you. And vice-versa, you will feel more responsibility, involvement, and gratitude, if you know them. People are more likely to respond to you and are more willing to help you beyond their responsibility if they know you, than if they don't know you.

People work with people, not machines. Know and understand the inter-dependencies between you and others, even outside of your circle.

Ideally the organizational chart is customized and edited throughout your career. Make sure you keep expanding it as you take on more roles. As you work with different teams or groups of people, keep adding them to your organizational chart. You can easily refer to people on the chart when someone asks you something that you don't know, or when you have a question of your own.

Once you gain experience and become a manager, present the chart to your subordinates so that they can look at the company as a big picture too.

14. Spend One Long Day in Your First Month at the Office

This is similar to the idea from the previous page. When you spend a long day at the office, you see the big picture over a period of time. Then you know better when people are available. Be the first person to come to the office and the last person to leave the office, then you can see who the early birds are and who the night owls are.

I consider the organizational chart from the previous page as three dimensional. People you work with in the same department (1st dimension), people who are in your department but who don't work with you directly (2nd dimension), and people in different departments (3rd dimension). Being present for a full workday will allow you to see how the company operates from the beginning to the end (Time = 4th dimension).

Combining the organizational chart and the time dimension will create a complete picture of the company. This will allow you know who does what and when they are available, which is crucial if your position requires coordination and collaboration.

Being able to catch key individuals makes a difference in your productivity and effectiveness.

Another benefit is that you can see when your productivity dramatically is decreased in a long day. Is it around the 10th or 12th hour when you hit a wall? Knowing your limit at work, you can be more productive. It's better to just go home, get extra rest and come in early the next day than trying to get everything done unproductively in a long day.

Your time is limited. Use it wisely.

There are days you work extra hours to get it done. Seasonality may be a part of the nature of your work. You have to adjust your working hours accordingly. But in general, it is wise to know your limit and work based on your best natural productivity in the long run.

15. Network, Network, Network!

The top three the most important aspects of real estate are location, location, location. I say the top three most important aspects of real world performance are network, network, network.

Networking starts anywhere and anytime, not just in a conference or at work. You always have an opportunity to meet new people throughout the day. At a coffee shop, in an airplane, or wherever, just smile and say hi to start a conversation!

Yes, I'm one of those people who talks to strangers on an airplane. Why? Well simply, the answer is that people are interesting. Everyone you meet knows something you don't know. I think of people as living Wikipedia, from whom I can learn many things. One stranger was a retired CPA who taught me a few tax tips, (that's always nice to know). Another one was an architect who traveled from California to Florida every other week. He offered me a place to stay if I ever went to CA (though I never had a chance to go). I even got a job offer one time. Interestingly I haven't had a bad experience talking to strangers. It always turns out to be positive ones.

There was an experiment to see how people felt after they had a conversation with strangers sitting next to them in public. The result was there was a more positive outcome talking to strangers just like my experience.

Don't get me wrong though. I don't say hi to everyone in sight like Crocodile Dundee in NYC. If I happen to be next to someone, that's when I say hi. Especially during a long travel day, I try to speak to at least one person. This is the best way to kill time!!

I know it's difficult the first time. But it can be as easy as saying hi.

You may feel uncomfortable at first. You are not alone in that. Despite only good outcomes, I still get nervous breaking the ice. Fortunately, talking to strangers is a skill like riding a bicycle. The more you do it, the easier it gets. For those who don't know where to start, just say hi and make a positive comment on something the person is wearing or carrying.

Many people like to talk about what they like or have a passion about. I know it's difficult the first time. But it can be as easy as saying hi. You never know. You might end up meeting someone who becomes special to you one day.

16. Think like an Employer rather than an Employee

This is similar to seeing the big picture at a macro level in the earlier pages but from a different point of view. What if you were the employer for your company, what kind of person would you (as the employer) want for the position that you (the future employee) want to have in the future? Goal-oriented? Optimistic? Innovative? Creative? Inspiring? Or Social?

You got hired (or will be hired) because your employer saw potential in you. If you were hiring someone, what would you look for in that person?

The key is to picture yourself not in your current position, but in the future position. The ultimate questions come down to:

    1. What do you want to be and do?
    2. What characteristics should you have when you are in that ideal position?

You should spend some time on both questions. The answer to question 1 will be critical for your future; you need to answer it as soon and as completely as possible. The skills and attitudes that you discover when you answer question 2 will take time to develop. Answer that question as soon as you can and then start investing effort in developing those skills. Also, your answers will change a little over time. Feel free to rethink your answers as your life changes, but not too often.

Your active time is limited. Knowing your ultimate goal takes you there most efficiently.

Think about this for a second. Life is like a maze with multiple paths, and you'll have to make decisions from time to time. Try to get from "Now" to "B", for example in the maze below. It might take you a few minutes to figure it out. But if you already know you want to end up at "B", then go backwards. It should take a few seconds rather than a few minutes to figure this out.

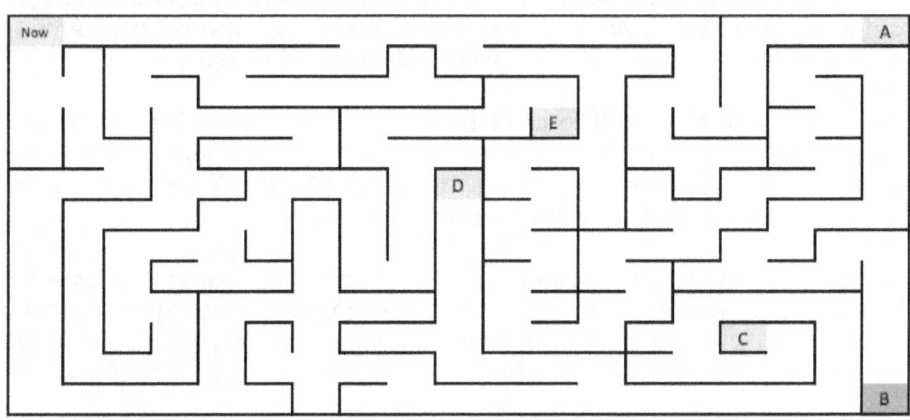

17. The Early Bird Gets the Worm

Twitter, Snapchat, Instagram... there are so many apps that capture your moments. Don't lie - you know you love the ping or buzz from your cell phone, right? When can you find 2 hours of your day without anyone bothering you? For most people, the answer is never.

The 2 hours a day though, makes a huge difference in your life if you can find it. This is the most productive time to get some work done. The question is how to make the time.

These non-distracted hours aren't created without sacrifice, yet it's worth it. Yes, you get up from the comfy bed early enough to make the 2 hours. I know the night owls hate the idea. The truth is no one is born to be a morning person. Most of the early birds did not have the habit of getting up early, but they do now. Why? It's simple. They CREATED the habit because they knew the benefit of the non-distracted hours.

Imagine you get up early and go to work as the first person every day. Spend the non-distracted hours to work on your projects or priorities. Your brain is fresh and clear. Your creativity and productivity are at their top gear. By the time others show up, you have done huge chunks of quality work. How would you feel then? I bet you'd feel great, right?

Another benefit is that your action speaks louder than your words. Your managers will like your enthusiasm, commitment and discipline by showing up as the first person. They'll like it more when you show them your quality work, too.

Sense of superiority becomes sense of confidence.

By showing up as the first person at work, you'll feel a sense of superiority. Having the quality work done during the non-distracted hours boosts your confidence. Very soon, you will have built yourself a great reputation among co-workers and managers. All you have to do is to get up early.

That being said, the sacrifice can't be avoided. Your night life will be less frequent. (You still have to have some night life, too; work and life balance is important.) You may have to give up some of your Netflix TV series. There will be less time to do your social media (thank me later).

The first week of adjusting to your new schedule is the hardest. It takes some time to change your internal clock. My suggestion is that you start this habit on the day we gain one hour from Daylight Saving time. One hour is given. You just have to make up one more hour.

Here is another benefit of getting up early. You can certainly avoid the traffic, assuming you drive to work!! The less time you spend in the car, the more time you have for whatever else you choose!

18. Don't Multi-task but Learn How to Deal with Multiple Tasks

You might have read research articles that blamed multi-tasking for inefficiency and lower achievement levels. It takes more time to complete multiple tasks by multi-tasking than finishing one at a time. The bottom line is that the brain is not built for multi-tasking.

The word "Multi-tasking" comes from computers performing several tasks at the same time. Computers can do that. They let you listen to music while you are typing some papers for your English Class. No problem.

Our brains however, can't handle many cognitively complicated tasks at the same effectively. I can prove that to you by asking you to read two books at the same time. Not possible.

Yet, we can walk and talk or play a guitar and sing at the same time. Isn't that multitasking? Yes, it is. The brains can handle multitasking when the activities become your second nature.

No matter how often you text every day, Driving and Texting at the same time are NOT and will NOT become your second nature!

Once you start your job, you'll have to learn how to juggle a list of tasks daily. Your brain will be overloaded with tons of information and new knowledge. The truth is that we know multi-tasking is not efficient, but we still have to deal with multiple tasks at the same time. The following will help you do better.

- **Prioritize your task list, then do one task at a time, from at or near the top of the list.** It's recommended that you ask your managers who the audience of your work is and what the timeline of the task is upon receiving it.

- **Make a to-do list for next day before you leave work.** You are most likely more productive in the morning since your brain is fresh and ready to go. Try to use that time for working on tasks rather than thinking about what to do on that day. That's a waste of quality time.

- **Give your brain a rest by switching to a different kind of task once you finish one.** For example, after you complete one task that requires heavy brain use, find a physical task to do such as organizing files or delivering papers to co-workers. By switching to a different kind of task, the brain will recover and become efficient again for the next round of tasks.

19. Have an Exit Strategy

I hope your first job fulfills the purpose of your life and allows you live happily after. It certainly can happen. But, it's more likely that your first job is just a stepping stone to bigger and better opportunities.

There is nothing wrong with that. People do change jobs every few years at the beginning to gain as much experience as possible and become well rounded. If you start off as a right fielder in baseball, don't you want to try a center fielder? How about a shortstop or pitcher?

Truth is that companies expect high turn-over in entry level jobs. That is the nature of lower-level positions.

The key is to keep your eye on the companies you want to work for one day. Also, if possible, meet the people from the companies and network. Insider information is much more reliable than Indeed.com. You might find out about an opening from them that is not publicly listed yet.

Maximize your personal and professional growth by jumping on opportunities and taking some risks even if you are happy where you are for the moment.

When you leave the current company for the next opportunity, make sure to be someone whom the current company will miss. Having a great relationship with prior employers is very important. You never know what may happen in your life. You might end up going back to the previous company.

20. To Leave or Not Leave?

There are always pros and cons in any decisions that we have to make. Hopefully you make a right choice that suits your situation.

Based on a research, the majority of people will not stay in one company during their career these days. You are most likely to leave your first job and move onto another within the first 5 years like stepping stones. There is nothing wrong with that. You do get exposed to different environments and acquire unique knowledge to become more well-rounded and more marketable to other companies for better opportunities.

At the same time, don't leave just because the grass looks greener in another job. Much of the information you can see is filtered, meaning that you only see what they want you to see. The worst thing would be for you to leave the current company and wish you would have stayed.

Another important thing is, before you leave, to make sure you become irreplaceable so that your current employer wants you to stay. Keeping a good relationship with your former employers is very important since you never know what opportunities will come up in the future.

Needless to say, if the current job makes your life miserable or devastates your health, I hope you can leave there immediately.

That being said, there are many pros to staying in one company, too. Your loyalty, for example, means a lot to the company. If many people stay in the company for many years, it's a good sign that the company is doing something right.

What I missed the most was the people I worked with when I left my first job. As I mentioned before, my first few years in the real world were challenging. It certainly made me stronger (what doesn't kill you makes you stronger, right?). What I was thankful for was the people, co-workers, and leaders, who helped me survive the tough times and grow into a better person.

So, what's the answer? Although obviously it depends on your situation, I have one general rule.

If you can't get where you want to be – Leave.
If you CAN get where you want to be – Stay.

Once you know what your life work is and where you want to be in the future, the question to leave or not to leave becomes clearer to you. I believe it's beneficial if you can share that information with your employers. They'll probably be honest with you about whether you are in the right place or not.

CHAPTER 2: RELATIONSHIP/SOCIAL INTERACTIONS

Living in a multi-cultural country, it's fascinating to see how many different relationships people have among their family, friends, co-workers, and society at large. Although many factors impact their relationships such as culture, religion, generation, gender, work, there is at least one thing in common - relationships are highly correlated with your level of happiness. The better relationships you have with others, the happier you are.

Although this section is meant to be about your first year in the real world, it's also good for any given time throughout your life. Relationships can be the biggest contributor to your survival in your first year at work.

21. Unwind and Live Simple

It's become a national stereotype that Millennials have a difficult time dealing with other people. Their relationships with friends and co-workers are superficial. When it comes to romance, fewer of them are in long-term, committed relationships than in previous generations.

Online dating has been getting more popular recently, which means there is less chance of "Love at first sight". I can't blame the online dating sites since, according to studies, 54% of online daters seriously misrepresent themselves in their profile. Who falls in love with fake photos??

You might believe having as many options as possible is a good thing, right? But then, you might suffer from the anxiety called FOMO, Fear of Missing Out. That's when you get so many options that you become overwhelmed. You start to **always** think that there must be better options, and then you find yourself afraid of missing those options. This keeps you from being present and enjoying where you actually are. One study shows that the more people you meet or see, the more overwhelmed you become. Then you tend to judge more superficially. The problem is that you start thinking there is always someone better out there for you, and you may be Missing Out on them.

Text is the primary mode of communication for Millennials. But with text, so much can get lost in translation. There is no tone or emotion to it. It's easy to misinterpret them.

These concerns are just the tip of the iceberg. But if you can't see a light at the end of the tunnel, there might be one solution for you.

Unwind whatever you do and live simple.

If you haven't been successful in online dating and it's getting stressful, simply quit. Meet someone somewhere else besides through fake pictures. If you feel FOMO, eliminate options by prioritizing what you really need or want. If you fear that you communicate poorly, talk more in person and don't rely on texting.

Another tip is to leave your cell phone home and go out all day. That may be hard at first, but if you stick to it, you will begin to feel less tied up and anxious.

22. Slow and Steady Wins the Race... Very Rarely

Building good relationships is not an overnight thing. It takes some time and effort. However, it takes only a few seconds to ruin a good relationship. I know it's not fair! But that's why we need to consider them seriously.

Remember the old story of The Tortoise and The Hare from your childhood? Here is a quick review just in case. A rabbit and turtle wanted to decide who was faster. As they started off the race, the rabbit quickly developed a huge lead. Soon he realized he was way ahead of the turtle, so he stopped to take a nap. By the time he woke up, the turtle had passed him by and won the race by moving slowly but steadily. The moral of the story is that slow and steady wins the race.

A relationship is like a race. You can approach it like the rabbit - fast but not consistent. Or you can approach it like the turtle - slow and steady. As you may guess, the relationship you build like the turtle is more powerful and meaningful in the real world.

Have you ever wondered though, if every race would end up with a turtle winning? Probably not. The probability of a rabbit falling asleep during the race would be very small. The Rabbit would most likely win the next 10 races in a row if they raced again. What's crazy is that the moral of the story is based on a very rare outcome of the event. Can we put our faith on that rare outcome? I can't. I'd prefer the rabbit over the turtle every time. The rabbit can win the race by being fast **and** consistent a lot more often than the turtle wins. I think the real moral of the story is that being consistent or steady is what really wins the race.

Also, have you ever wondered why the turtle would agree to run a race in the first place? Why wouldn't he suggest a biathlon (run and swim)? Wouldn't it be fairer to him? So, what's the moral here? Choose your Race!

Last of all, why would they even have to compete against each other? Couldn't they help each other and finish the race together? The rabbit could help the turtle on the land, and the turtle could help the rabbit in the water. The time to finish the race together would be much faster, and the chance of finishing the race would be much greater than if they compete against each other in the race.

Fast, consistent, and reliable beats slow and steady every time.

What does the story tell us? I believe building relationship slowly and steadily is good. Building a relationship fast and consistent is better. Building a relationship fast, consistent, and reliable beats them all. And if you can, choose your relationships too.

23. Say Goodbye to Social Anxiety

Recall how in your first year of high school or college you met a lot more new people then than the rest of school combined. Well it's déjà vu - you are meeting a lot of new people again. Some people don't mind it at all. But some do mind it because they have the social anxiety. People with social anxiety don't feel comfortable around new people and can't hold a conversation for a long time. Also, it tires them out easily.

I know how that feels. I used to have minor social anxiety. I felt meeting new people and chitchatting with them sucked. The thought of talking in a group discussion gave me chills and even nightmares.

But at some point, I realized that meeting new people and chatting with them is a skill that anyone can acquire, just like riding a bicycle.

At first, it's scary. If you don't practice often, it stays scary. Once you have enough practice though, it will become more natural. But you need game plans. You can't ride and fall every time till suddenly magic happens and you can ride. That may not happen; (it only happens for a handful people). You prevent yourself from falling by using training wheels or having someone hold the bicycle for you. Sometimes it is a great idea to break it down into smaller activities, like balancing and pedaling. You can even remove the pedals temporarily so that you can just focus on balancing first.

How about meeting new people and chatting? Of course, there are many game plans for those. However, just a few can make the difference. I use only the two rules below.

- **Speak the person's Name Three Times within 30 Seconds**: One of the reasons why some people have a tough time talking to a new person is that they can't hold a conversation because they don't remember the new person's name. By repeating the name three times within the first 30 seconds after you meet a new person, the name will stick in your head while the conversation is going on. Also, if the name relates to someone you already know, make a connection between them. For example, if I meet someone named Taylor, ask them if they like Karaoke. If yes, that's a connection to Taylor Swift! If not, ask if they like any vampire series. If yes, that's a connection to Taylor Lautner (Jacob Black in the Movie Twilight), and so on.

- **Prepare Open-Ended Questions in Advance**: When you meet a new person, your brain is working hard to remember their name while processing the details of the conversation. Let's reduce the brain use by having some questions prepared in advance. For example, I have a set of 10 questions to ask new people every time so that I don't have to think what to ask next. They don't have to be fancy at all, and they are very handy. Some of the questions are as simple as "How did you like your school?" or "What is your hobby?" Once you find something in common, then you can drop the rest of the prepared questions and talk about only that subject.

As I mentioned before, this is a skill that anyone can acquire. However, it requires practice. I have overcome my social anxiety after much practice of the above two rules. Now I actually enjoy meeting new people because they are fascinating. At a coffee shop, in restaurants, or on an airplane, I say hi and use the prepared questions to chat with them. This section leads to the next one - Meet People.

24. Meet People

Again, this is not only for the first year of your school or the real world. You should continue meeting people throughout your life both within your professional environment and privately. We are social animals and can't live by ourselves. Our lives are always dependent on others. It's interesting that the symbol for "people" in Japanese is only two lines, but those two lines look as though they are holding one another up, each propped against the other. This is what we do as people – we support one another.

When the number of your Twitter or Instagram followers increases, don't you feel happier? One of the four brain chemicals that are responsible of making us feel happy is called oxytocin. It is associated with empathy, trust, sexual activity, and relationship-building. When we meet new people or get more followers, that chemical is released in our brains and helps us to become more social creatures. The more you meet people and build relationships, the happier you feel.

It's easier said than done though. As I mentioned in the previous sections - it can be as easy as saying "Hi". Make sure to have your prepared questions ready and remember the people's names. Discover their passions and ask about them. That's all. Next thing you know oxytocin is released in their brains. You can't see that, of course, but you can tell because they will seem happy talking about their passions.

Also, be prepared to be surprised by people. In general, people are amazing. They have unique experiences, knowledge, and stories, that are different from yours. Ask to share them with you. You might find it very interesting.

The follow up is important, too. If appropriate, ask them to become friends on social media. Leave some comments like "It was nice meeting you". Ask if you can do something together or help them out in any way. That's a fast, consistent and reliable relationship building method.

It's not whom you know but who knows you.

That new relationship will be handy one day when you need some help. The people you know may not be able to help you. For example, you know Derek Jeter, the former captain of the NY Yankees. But he won't teach you how to field ground balls, assuming he doesn't know you. What matters the most is who knows you. In other words, he would teach you if he knew you.

There are always pros and cons in everything, right? Sorry I lied. I can't think of any cons to meeting people. If you can think of any, please leave me a message or comment and become friends on my Facebook account (Yes, oxytocin to me!!).
The bottom line is when you meet people and build a good relationship, good

things will happen whether you anticipate them or not. I landed my first job because someone knew me. I didn't get to know him, hoping he'd give me a job. It just happened that way.

25. Reconnect with Your Old Network

The previous section focuses on new people. This section, on the other hand, focuses on people you already know.

It may seem counterintuitive since you are either starting or just started a new job. In fact, you may feel so busy with your new job, new people, and new life, that you may not feel you have time for people from your past.

But what I mean by reconnecting with your old network doesn't take much time. It's as simple as asking how your old mentors or friends are doing and telling them how things are going in your new life in a quick email or text. If possible, having a cup of coffee or drinks with them once in a while does the job.

Keeping your old professional and personal network active has multiple benefits. First, exchanging information is always a plus. Although you are not currently searching for jobs, you may hear about other interesting opportunities for the future. Second, as I mentioned in the previous section, your old network is not just some people you know. They also know you. If you actively keep up a good relationship with them, your future self will thank you for it.

The energy and effort you have invested in people will pay off significantly at a time when you don't expect it.

I reconnect with my old network once in a while over a cup of coffee or drinks. Since I am more math oriented than linguistic, I'm thankful to have a friend from my previous job who is able to help me to write this book. I know my strengths and weaknesses. Having a good relationship can fill in where I lack.

26. Social Media can Ruin Your Job

"We human beings are social beings. We come into the world as the result of others' actions. We survive here in dependence on others. Whether we like it or not, there is hardly a moment of our lives when we do not benefit from others' activities. For this reason, it is hardly surprising that most of our happiness arises in the context of our relationships with others." – Dalai Lama

Humans are indeed social animals. We love to know what other people's businesses are. It's just human nature. For some careers, networking and being social are major components of the job.

It's important, however, to draw a line between your professional social life and your personal social life!

My editor can agree with me on this. Once the line disappears or moves in the wrong direction, you'll lose control of your professional and personal opinions, which can cause huge career risks. People do lose their jobs because of their social posts.

What if your manager sends you a friend request on Facebook? That is a good debate question. If your Facebook page is for personal reasons, I suggest you do not add them. But if your Facebook page exits for professional reasons, then do add them. You can create a professional social media page in Linked In or somewhere else and add them to that instead of your personal social media. In this way, you can keep the line between your professional and personal social lives. The last thing you want to show the managers is a picture of you passed out on the street on your birthday with your drinking buddies.

I have been relieved since the moment I deleted my Facebook page.

There is an interesting article about how much time people spend on social media during their life time. According to the study run by the marketing agency Mediakix, the average time spent per day on social media is the following:

YouTube = 40 min
Facebook = 35 min
Snapchat = 25 min
Instagram = 15 min
Twitter = 1 min

People spend about 2 hours a day in social media! The accumulated amount is over 5 years of your life. Please note that this is a snapshot of our current average. Since social media has been exponentially growing during the last 15 years, with no sign of slowing, the amount of time spent on social media will most likely increase in the future.

Again, I know we are social animals. I only suggest going easy on social medial while you are at work.

27. We are Addicted to Cell Phones and Social Media

Addiction – the fact or condition of being addicted to a particular substance, thing or activity; dependency; compulsion; enslavement; obsession.
People with addiction are unable to control the use of a habit-forming substance or activity, or to forego an unhealthy habit.

Does this sound familiar to you? No, I'm not talking about drugs, alcohol, tobacco, gambling, or video games here. I'm talking about something you do every day, every hour, perhaps each minute - Cell phone and social media use.

Do you check your cell phone without realizing it? When you see something cool, do you immediately think about posting it on social media? Do you feel worried or uneasy without a cell phone? If the answer to any of these questions is yes, then most likely you are addicted.

I don't blame you. I believe most people are addicted to it whether they admit it or not.

How did we become addicted then?

When you get a text message, or someone leaves a comment on a social media, a chemical called dopamine is released in your brain. That's the same chemical that is released when you do drugs, drink alcohol, or play video games. The chemical makes you feel good but is also highly addictive.

Sometimes, we don't need anyone to respond to our text or leave social media comments to get a shot of dopamine. A Harvard research scientist reported in 2012, that talking about oneself through social media activates a pleasure sensation (dopamine) in the brain.

The problem for any addiction is withdrawal. We get depressed, unhappy, and stressed. Then we go back to our cell phone or social media and try to get more shots of dopamine. It's a death spiral. The issue becomes deeper and deeper.

Also, there is a study that shows the time we spend on a social media is correlated with how depressed we become in everyday life.

Cell phone use and social media is never a solution to whatever problem you have and is not appropriate for certain situations.

I'll get deeper into that subject in the next section. Meanwhile, I want to make one thing very clear - Cell phone and social media use is not a bad thing per se. But excessive use **is** a bad thing. It's just like drinking alcohol or playing a video game. Doing a little bit of those is not a bad thing. In fact, having a glass of wine each day is good for you. Playing a video game for a short time reduces stress.

That being said, let's talk more about when cell phone and social media use is not appropriate.

28. Invisible Wall

It's safe to claim that a cell phone is too important for some people to live without. Many things can be done instantly in the palms of our hands. There are over one hundred thousand apps available to stimulate our brains and entertain us. You probably can't imagine a bus ride without having a cell phone.

There is absolutely nothing wrong with that at all. I do it too when I ride a bus or train if it's an everyday ride, though not so much during a vacation.

Do you notice though, that a cell phone creates an invisible wall between you and others? Imagine Person A comes and asks Person B for help while Person B is texting. Person B may be listening and giving sound advice. However, Person A automatically senses that "You are not my priority" before Person A hears the advice. This same effect can occur even if Person B is only **holding** a cell phone. It's difficult for Person A to build a good relationship with Person B with that attitude.

And body language speaks volumes, (I'll cover that in more detail in a later section). If Person B's body is not facing towards Person A, it signifies "You are not my priority". Again, it's difficult to build a good relationship with that attitude.

Do you put your cell phone on the table at dinner or in a meeting? If so, you are unconsciously giving a sign of "You are not my priority" to the others. By the way, putting it upside down doesn't mean anything to the others. The problem is that you may not be aware how the others feel when they see your cell phone between you and them. The next thing you know, your cell phone buzzes, and everyone sees you paying attention to the message. Basically, it doesn't matter how serious the conversation you and the others are having. You show that your priority is a message on your cell phone, not the people at the table or in the meeting. Again, it's difficult to build a good relationship with that attitude.

Remove the wall!

This is a true story. A father spent 90 minutes with his family every night at their dinner table. Because he valued the family time, he made sure to come home in time for dinner and spend that time. The problem was that he had his laptop and cellphone on the table while eating with his family. One day he had some issues and couldn't come home in time for dinner.

When he arrived home, there were only 20 minutes left before his daughter's bed time. He dropped everything then and spent the next 20 minutes with her, no laptop or cellphone nearby. She woke up next morning and asked his father to come home **late** again. Suddenly he realized that he had an invisible wall between him and his family every night. Every night that is, **except** for the night before.

If you want to build good relationships, the first step is to show your full attention 100% to the people around you by putting your cell phone somewhere they can't see and by facing your body towards them. Don't underestimate those small things because small things can make big differences especially in relationships.

29. Communication is the Foundation of Building Good Relationships

Not long ago, I started seeing families sitting at restaurant tables with their kids playing on their cell phones rather than being in conversation with their families. I understand why they do it. It's so easy and convenient to have the kids occupied with something so that the parents get a little break.

As I mentioned before, there are always pros and cons in any decisions. Parents sometimes want a break from their kids. Giving the kids cell phones does that job beautifully. But what about the cons? Is there any long term effect from the decision to give them cell phones and not require them to interact with their family?

TV dinner is somewhat similar to that situation. That's where the whole family eats meals while watching TV. I admit that I grew up like that. But to be honest, I wish my family hadn't allowed that.

I had a chance to live with another family for a year. In that family they sat at a dinner table and talked instead of watching TV. Their kids' communication level far exceeded mine. I wondered why my communication level was poor for many years till one day someone told me that all I did was listen and not speak. Strangely I still remember that moment vividly. It was then I realized that watching TV at the dinner table enabled me to merely listen and not speak. In other words, I was never required to learn how to communicate at the dinner table with my own family.

Things can get ugly with excessive texting on a date. In 2017, an Austin man filed a suit against his date, alleging that she had been texting during the movie on their date and owed him the price of a ticket ($17.31). During a media interview with him, he talked about the practice of texting in public and the poor behavior of his date. According to her though, she chose to end their date prematurely since she felt uncomfortable, and she needed to remove herself from the situation. Her solution was to give him a sign of "let's end this date" by texting excessively.

It seemed that the bad experience started with his misbehavior and led to her excessive texting. How could this ugliness have been avoided? Probably she wouldn't have texted so much if he treated her better. But she also failed to communicate with him.

How to end a date properly is just as important as how to continue one.

The truth is that we all have had a bad date or two (or even more) in our lives. She assumed he'd pick up on her sign, and he didn't. Perhaps she could have said something like "I am having a good time but I'm sorry - I have to go due to emergency". Then her bad night would've been over.

Although you may not think it's wrong or inappropriate to use a cell phone when you are accompanied, try to avoid using it at the dinner table, in a meeting, or at friend's house where you are with others. Try instead to really **be** in the presence of those whom you are with. You can use the cell phone or text later. But you can talk to people face to face only when you are with those people.

30. Men Love Their Man Caves; Women Love Their Girl Friends

When I could afford only a one bed room apartment or a studio, living there with someone else was very stressful. I felt the need to be alone from time to time. I drove my car around town by myself often to create my alone time rather than going home. When we moved to a two-bed room apartment, I converted one of the rooms into my office. It was far from being a "Man Cave" but it was good enough to provide me with a space. I didn't realize that I spent my time there alone quite often till my wife pointed it out.

As I paid more attention to my behavior, I found a pattern. I wasn't trying to avoid her, which was her claim. Instead, I went to my office or drove my car alone whenever I felt stressed. It turned out some of my male friends agreed with me that they'd do the same.

A Man Cave is a place to relieve stress from work and life.

Since my smart phone is almost 2 years old, the battery barely keeps a charge till the end of the day. Although I can use it just fine, it needs some juice during the day to survive. People are like cell phones. We need to get recharged once in a while to last for a long day. For men, a man cave is not only a place to relieve stress but also to recharge mentally by turning off the brain power. Men who are recharged and coming out of their man cave tend to respect, care for, understand, and listen to others more than before.

What about women? Although they do like a space for themselves such as a big walk-in closet full of beautiful clothes and shoes, women's preference to reduce their stress and to recharge themselves is different than men's. Women in general like to meet and chat with their female friends.

I often encourage my wife to go have a girl's night or a lunch with her friends, promising that I will do all the house work while she is gone. Meanwhile, she lets me stay in my office and do whatever when I need a little time off from reality.

Maintaining stress levels within a reasonable range will allow us to focus on what's really important in life.

Disclaimer: obviously everyone is different. There are some men who would rather talk with their friends to reduce stress. And there are some women who would rather stay in their woman cave playing video games to reduce stress. The bottom line is that you should at least know your partner's preference so that you can offer an appropriate suggestion just like my offer to my wife that she should go out with her friends and enjoy herself.

31. Give What the Other Person Wants, Not What You Want the Other Person to Have

Have you ever given a gift and the recipient's reaction was not as expected, even though you thought you purchased a perfect gift for that person? The result was that they were disappointed, and you were frustrated.

It's happened to me many times. I spent a lot of time thinking about a perfect gift and gave it to her. All I heard was one word - "Thanks".

Holidays, Birthdays, Anniversaries... there are many occasions throughout a year to celebrate. For each occasion, you have a year to come up with a perfect gift or gifts. It seems like plenty of time to prepare. Truth is, it doesn't matter how long you have to prepare, if you don't know what your recipient really wants in the first place. Sure, you can shoot blindly and hope you hit the bullseye. Unfortunately, you are unlikely to get it right because your unconscious bias applies to the gift that you purchase. In other words, you tend to buy things that you want your partner to have, not what your partner wants to have.

Some may say that it's just a part of relationship building. Some may say it's a test of how well you know your partner. Apparently, I did poorly in building a relationship with her and certainly failed the test... ouch!

If you are like I was, here is some advice for you - Just ask what they want in advance.

You may argue that it ruins the surprise and defeats the purpose of giving a gift. Not too fast, my friend. You buy what they want as a backup and buy what you think is a perfect gift as a primary. On the special day, give them the backup first to meet the expectation. Then give your primary to go beyond. You may hear one word "Thanks" for your primary gift, but the back-up guarantees you real appreciation.

Save time, money, and feelings by asking

There are times you have to shoot blindly. For example, if they say "oh I don't want anything" then you have very little information for what to buy. If an open-ended question doesn't work, switch it to a "which would you rather have?" question. That'll give you some hint of what to buy. Gifts are physical things. They're relatively easy to give as long as you know what to give. It gets much more complicated when it comes to non-physical things such as emotions. The next section will go over that.

32. Emotional Needs

What a girl wants, what a girl needs,
Whatever makes me happy and sets you free.
And I'm thanking you for knowing exactly
what a girl wants...
Christina Aguilera

In 1995, psychologist and science journalist Daniel Goleman published a book introducing the concept of Emotional Intelligence to the world. This idea, the idea that an ability to understand and manage emotions greatly increases our chances of success, greatly influences the way people now think about emotions and human behavior.

Emotional Intelligence can be measured by answering a series of questions. The results of the test are often referred as EQ, (like IQ but for emotion instead of intellect). If you have a high EQ score, Christina Aguilera would thank you for "knowing exactly". For those who don't have high scores (like me), things can be very frustrating, like giving a gift that is not appreciated as much as you expect.

When it comes to emotions, you really can't ask what the other person wants when the person's demand changes quite often. What worked last time may not work this time. Also, you definitely need to give what the person wants, not what you want the other person to have.

And this is all complicated further by demographic groups such as gender or age which play a huge role in deciding what to give.

The book *Men are from Mars, Women are from Venus* by John Gray, published in 1992, has a general list of people's emotional wants by sex or gender.

	Emotional Needs for Women	Emotional Needs for Men
1	Caring	Trust
2	Understanding	Acceptance
3	Respect	Appreciation
4	Devotion	Admiration
5	Validation	Approval
6	Reassurance	Encouragement

When I saw this list, I was very excited, like a porcupine seeing a pineapple for the first time (from Family Guy). This was because I finally figured out why my wife's response was not as expected when I gave her my trust, acceptance, and appreciation. In fact, I gave her what I wanted, not what she wanted, which were caring, understanding, and respect.

Again, those who have a high EQ score may be able to naturally provide what the other wants emotionally. For those whose EQ is lower, this list is a good start when trying to take an appropriate action. It certainly helps me!

33. Make Your Good Habits Your Routines!

When you wake up in the morning, you do the morning routine such as taking a shower, brushing your teeth, and getting dressed without much thought about it. Your routine has become automated. What's awesome about automation is that it reduces the need for brain usage throughout the day. It allows you to spend your energy efficiently and to focus on what's really important. I have created many automations at work, where all I had to do is to press a button, then a few seconds later my work was done. Without these automations, I would have spent a much longer time to do the same work while having to use my energy and brain power.

If you have a partner, have as many good habits turn into your routines as possible. For example, if you have a female partner, open a door for her, buy her flowers weekly, and just listen to her for 15 min every day without interrupting her. If you have a male partner, encourage him in what he wants to accomplish, write a thank you note weekly, and leave him alone for 15 min every day without interrupting him.

Imagine your days when your emotional needs are continually fulfilled because your partner does it automatically!

Your stress level will likely be stable. You will have more energy to focus on other things. It will be much easier to deal with issues when they arise while you are in this good condition. It sounds like a win-win scenario, doesn't it?

Making your habits your routine takes some time. It takes a few weeks, months, or even longer. It also drains your energy and requires your thoughts at first till it becomes automatic. But think of this as your investment. You spend all of that on the front end. Then, once your acts have become habits, you benefit from these habits without even thinking about them. Another example is exercise. There will be days you don't want to go for many reasons. But once you get to the point where exercise is your daily or weekly routine, you get benefits from it without noticing, such as stress management, weight management, and healthy life style.

I believe it is very powerful to have routines in your relationships. The longer you are in the same relationship, the more you tend to forget to do good things for each other. One of my favorite routines is to hold my wife's hand or kids' hands when we are in public. I'm creating a family bond without even thinking about it.

You may think of routines as activities that you do within short time periods, such as daily, weekly, or monthly. If they become something you and your partner do together once in a great while, such as each year, you can call them your traditions. I'll cover that more in the next section.

34. Create Mini-traditions

Creating mini-traditions can nurture your relationships along the way since they become **your thing.** They don't have to be super fancy like going on international trips or renting a limousine a night. They can be as simple as going to a certain restaurant on your anniversary or curving pumpkins during the Halloween season. Start building a tradition that creates a meaningful purpose in your relationships.

The reason you want to start your tradition is to have something that both of you look forward to.

My wife and I started a tradition during the holiday season. We watch a movie called "Family Man" with Nicholas Cage. The movie demonstrates what's really important in one's life regardless of whether you're rich or not. We love the movie because it reminds us what to prioritize in our lives besides just money. It's a good annual reminder and makes us appreciate what we have as a family.

The seasons can help you build traditions for you and your partner.

Spring time:
> Baseball, visiting local flower gardens, picking berries, etc.

Summer time:
> Water activities, taking trips during summer break, Renting a beach house, etc.

Fall time:
> Football games, Trail hiking, running marathons, Hunting, etc.

Winder time:
> Skiing or snowboarding, Basketball, holiday activities, visit NYC to watch The Ball drop, etc.

Having mini-traditions puts us in the next level of relationships. One holiday season, we almost missed watching the movie and felt very awkward and uneasy till we finally watched it at the end of the season. It felt like something important between us was missing. Also, watching it individually wouldn't have felt quite right. Because we watched it together and kept our tradition, it meant something to us.

For those who are having issues about any relationships including love relationships, friendships, or work relationships, create something with special meaning between you and your partners. This will help you to grow the relationships more and solve conflicts you may have.

35. Road Trips

As technology improves more and more, we become less and less patient. It seems the two are inversely correlated. We send text messages and expect the responses within a reasonable time frame. We even check our cellphones multiple times if people don't respond quickly. We are attracted to words such as "Fast results!" or "Immediate effects!". We are less interested otherwise. For example, you are more likely to sign up for a "Lose 5lbs in 3 days" diet rather than a "Lose 5lbs in 3 weeks" diet. Am I right? Wouldn't you take a "Lose 5lbs in 3 hours" magic pill if one existed? I would, assuming it was not a laxative.

As I mention previously, building relationships takes time. We must spend time together over and over again to create rapport, trust, and reliability with each other. However, what if there is a magic pill that speeds up the process?

Well, it's not a pill but it's something to take. It's a **Road Trip**. For 10 years in a row, two of my friends and I went on a 7-day road trip every year. I knew one guy well but not the other one at first. As we spent more time together each year, our relationships grew stronger. After over 10 trips, I'm proud to call them my best friends.

When you meet someone new or start dating someone, you are hiding some parts of yourself so that they'll like you more. It's actually easier to be someone you're **not** if you meet someone once in a while. As you spend more time together, you can't continue to fake yourself, and you start showing who you really are. Does it sound familiar?

Road trips are a great way to get to know others, and a great opportunity for them to get to know you in short period of time.

Adventure Racing is typically a multi-disciplinary team sport involving navigation over an unmarked wilderness course, including running, climbing, paddling, mountain biking, horse riding, skiing, white water rafting, and more. Running a course can take from 2 hours to 11 days with the teammates trying to get to the goal from the middle of nowhere. Teams must travel together the entire race, usually within 150ft of each other for the whole time. Since each team navigates for themselves, completely on their own, one wrong move can cause a loss of hours or even days. In such harsh conditions, the participants say that trust is the most important factor during the race. Obviously, those who don't trust each other within a team will never finish the race.

But it doesn't have to be that extreme to get to know each other well and build relationships in ordinary times. The point is that by spending a long time together consecutively, such as on a road trip or Adventure Racing, you'll know whether the partner or friend is right for you.

If you just started seeing someone and aren't sure if they are The One, your Mr. or Ms. Right, I highly recommend you take a road trip together.

36. Bucket List

You might have created your own bucket list - a list of things to do in life before you die. But how about one with your partner? A bucket list with your partner is not only for fun and enjoyable but also for relationship building since some items require a lot of preparation, planning, and working together to cross off the items on the list.

Bucket lists give a double benefit - you get to enjoy the items two ways. One is to plan and the other is to actually do. Planning is a good communication exercise. You and your partner will practice communicating in a healthy and productive way. To do things on the list is a good relationship building exercise. You get to learn each other's strengths and weaknesses and learn to accommodate them by getting to know each other.

Here are some ideas -
   a. Volunteer together
   b. Complete a physical challenge such as running (5k, half or full marathon) or hiking parts of the Appalachian Trail
   c. Host and serve a Thanksgiving meal at your home
   d. Sign up for social dancing
   e. Take a cooking class together
   f. Horseback Ride on the beach
   g. Bungee Jump while holding each other's hands
   h. Complete a Jigsaw Puzzle together
   i. Get Chinese foot massages together
   j. Write a song together
   k. Dress up in matching costumes for Halloween
   l. Create a music playlist about your relationship
   m. Take a Hot Air Balloon ride
   n. Join the Mile-High Club
   o. Go Skinny Dipping
   p. Build a snow man together
   q. Dress up and go see a musical or classical concert
   r. Babysit together
   s. Make a time-capsule
   t. Write a love letter to each other
   u. Duet "Love is an Open Door" with your partner

A cool thing is that a bucket list with your partner is a visible representation of how much your relationship is growing. Also, the items in the list above are budget friendly. Certainly, if you want to, you can spend thousands of dollars to go on a Caribbean cruise to see the beautiful beaches or take a European trip to see different wineries. If you just started seeing your partner recently, you might want to go with the ones above rather than spending big $.

Ok, so you created a list and crossed off some of the items. Now what? It's time to talk about your ultimate goal with your partner. We'll cover that in the next section.

37. North Star

For thousands of years Polaris, the North Star, has been used as a guide and reference point for navigators, travelers, and astronomers. Because the northern axis of the earth points directly toward the North Star, it will always point to true north and help you find your direction even in the darkest of nights no matter where you are in the northern hemisphere.

Finding the North Star is simple. First find the Big Dipper (also called Ursa Major or The Big Bear in the US, and "the Saucepan" in many other countries). It's one of the most well-known groups of stars. It looks like a saucepan. Locate the two pointer stars that are at the end of the saucepan where liquid would run off if you tipped it up. The North Star will be always five times the distance between these two pointers proceeding upward from the saucepan.

A relationship is like traveling. When everything is going well, it's like traveling in NYC where all the streets are simply numbered like E 57th St or 5th Ave. You can figure out where you are now and how you get to where you want to go. You probably don't have to think about the North Star then. When things are more difficult and complicated in your relationship, it's like walking in the wilderness. You don't know where you are or where you should go.

That being said, the question that you want to ask yourself and your partner is "What is our North Star in our relationship that will allow us to find our direction when we are lost?"

Having a Northern Star in your relationship during the hard times will help you reset your mindset and start walking in the right direction.

You can think of a North Star as your ultimate goal between you and your partner. What will the future between you and your partner look like 50 years from now?

One day I saw a 70+ year old couple holding hands together taking a walk. At that moment, I found my North Star. That's where I want my wife and I to be someday.

Once I had that goal in my mind, our lives became simpler. I often ask myself a question; "How does this argument or frustration get me where I want to go?"

The answer usually is - it doesn't. And that means I have no reason to continue with this argument or to stay frustrated. Then I simply drop all my negative feelings and focus on positive things that will help me go towards my North Star. What really matters is not whether I win the argument but whether my wife and I will hold each other's hands in our 70s. It's that simple.
It's always easier to start with a long-term goal, and then work out periodic

checkpoints next, where you and your partner talk about how things are going. We'll cover that in the next section.

38. Strategic Meeting

When you declared your major in college, you didn't take 4-year worth of random classes and then suddenly declare your major right before graduation, right? You decided your major first and then set up your schedules each semester based on that major's requirements till your graduation, didn't you? Some of you might have already known what you wanted to become so deciding your major happened long before.

Just like in the previous section where you solved the maze backwards, knowing your ultimate goal and building your plan accordingly is much more efficient than trying to hit a target blindly.

If you haven't done so with your partner, now is the time to get together and ask each other one question. I call it The Miracle Question. This exercise is a great way for couples to explore the type of future they would like to build, individually and as a couple. Knowing both your and your partner's goals can aid you in understanding what each of you needs in order to be happy in the relationship. Here is the question.

Suppose tonight while you slept, a miracle occurred...
When you awake tomorrow, what would you become aware of that would tell you your life had suddenly gotten better? How would you know?

Once you establish the time with your partner to talk about the goal, schedule this strategic meeting in your calendar weekly, monthly, quarterly, or annually. Remove any distractions such as cellphones or work-related items. By the way, this is non-negotiable.

The topics might be different between a weekly meeting and an annual meeting. In the weekly meetings, you may talk with your partner about how you both are doing, your relationship as a couple, any unfinished arguments or grievances, or any needs that are not being met. The focus is about things that happened recently. The questions can be as simple as the following:
- How do you feel about us today?
- Is there anything that feels incomplete from this past week that you would like to talk about?
- How can I make you feel more loved in the coming days?

In the annual meeting, you may talk about your long-term goals and the progress towards them.

The answers to these questions should lead you and your partner in a healthy and productive discussion about yourselves and your relationship. Having Strategic Meetings regularly can help you and your partner keep on top of any issues and fix any cracks in your relationship as soon as possible.

39. The Art of Asking for Help from Your Partner

Do you have trouble asking your partner for help or telling them what to do? Do you get frustrated because either nothing gets done or your partner complains about your requests?

Let's talk about it from a Big Picture perspective rather than just between you and your partner. People in general are driven by their self-interest and trapped in their own wants, needs, and desires. They are not interested in your problems but are interested in what they can get in return. They'll do you a favor once or twice without expecting any returns. But eventually, they'll stop doing you favors unless you provide them with what they want. Does that sound familiar to you?

People do things because
    a.   They want something in return
    b.   They want to avoid the consequence of not doing something

Option a: If people are driven by their self-interest, why not include something in your request that could be in their interest? That can be done by finding out what your partner wants first.

For example, if you need laundry help, ask your partner what they want you to wear for your next date. Let them know that the clothes are in the laundry basket. Tell them that you'd love to wear the clothes and look good on your date, then ask them to do laundry for you.

Option b: When you ask your partner what to do, it's never a good idea to use the second option. Holding a knife and asking your partner to do laundry won't go well in the long term.

Also, it's never a good idea to remind your partner of your previous support and rely on their gratitude. Unfortunately, that's ineffective and ends up disappointing.

Always recall that your partner's stress level is inversely correlated with your success rate. The more stressed they are, the less chance your request will be granted. That's why "Emotional Needs" and "Make your Habits your Routine" in the previous sections matter daily.

I have a few tips to increase your success rate.

- Use the table in the previous section "Emotional Needs" to keep your partner's stress level down

- Use "Would you?' rather than "Could you?"

- Avoid immediate requests if possible. Give your partner some time to get it done

- Leave a thank-you note before it gets done since people forget about requests

- Pick your priority. You may get "No" this time but your next request will have a better chance

40. Relationships Require Continuous Education from Both Ends

We are life-long learners in relationships. There is no one set of rules that fit all kinds of relationships, and they change their demands from time to time. If you fail to realize the need for adaption, then your relationships can go down the toilet. In fact, you might want to pay more attention to those then your college classes because relationships matter to you more than anything.

Here are a few tips that can support your life-long learning and nurture your relationships.

- When your partner talks about stressful days, don't take it personally or don't give advice. Most of the time your partner just wants to express their feelings and thoughts. That's all. Turn your body toward them and listen to their stories. For the next few minutes, nod a few times and be a sandbag. It's always a good idea to give a hug afterwards.
- Make your partner feel like a priority
- Give compliments or a thank-you note daily
- Assume less and ask more

Another good tip when things are not going well is to write a love letter. It's a love letter so it needs to end with a positive and loving message, which is tough when you are angry and upset. Take your time and put your thoughts together in a way that your partner can follow. Start with positive facts such as *"Thank you for being a great partner for x years"* and *"you have been a light to my life"*. Follow with simple and clear messages or bullet points of what's bothering you. Always end positively such as *"Thank you again for understanding and being with me"*.

To start positively motivates your partner to read your thank-you letter. Putting down your thoughts simply and clearly in a letter gives your partner a chance to think about it longer and read it multiple times. To end positively makes your voice heard and enhances your relationship.

There will be times you and your partner have to agree to disagree. Two people, coming from two different places and having two different perspectives, of course will see the world differently. But remember that you can only see the 180 degrees in front of you by yourself. With your partner, both of you can see 360 degrees, the whole thing. Respect your partner's opinions.

The best relationships are ones in which both partners feel like the luckiest person in the world!

41. Female Brain vs Male Brain

I still have a hard time understanding why my wife can't read a map. When I explain directions, she pretends to listen to me and ends up using a GPS. But the tables do turn - she can multitask, but I can't.

It turns out there are two types of brains, Female brain and Male brain. One is not better than the other. Their strengths are simply in different fields.

There are studies about female behaviors by Ihoko Kurokawa, Female Brain Scientist. She claims that females raise babies who can't speak yet, so they excel at the ability to observe non-verbal signs and clues, which is an indication of love to females. On the other hand, Males have less of that ability. Although that does not mean males don't love, females may think they don't.

Have you ever experienced a female saying she'd do it by herself, but then getting angry after you left her alone? She probably gave many signs and clues indicating that she wanted you to do it, but you didn't read them correctly. If you run into that situation next time, just do it.

Don't say "I'd have done it if you had asked". She wants you to read her signs and clues. She wants you to do it without her having to tell you what to do. This phrase might cause her to believe you don't love her because you are not reading the signs and clues right.

Women are more inclined to combine logic and intuition

Another difference between a female brain and male brain is that the purpose of communication is to empathize for a female brain but to solve problems for a male brain. I'll cover three types of empathy in the next section.

42. Three Types of Empathy

Empathy begins with understanding life from another person's perspective. Nobody has an objective experience of reality. It's all through our own individual prisms. – Sterling Brown

Empathy is a must for any successful relationship. Daniel Goleman, psychologist who popularized the theory of emotional intelligence, talks about three different types of empathy.

- Cognitive Empathy

Cognitive empathy occurs when you think about situation from another person's point of view, as though you were in someone else's shoes. According to Goleman, cognitive empathy is awareness and understanding someone else's perspective, which is a crucial part of maintaining a good connection and communication.

- Social Empathy

Social empathy is to sense what the other person is feeling. By mirroring what you sense, you can create rapport with others.

- Empathic Concern

Empathic concern is the next step beyond empathy. This is when you give actual help. If you know someone who needs help in your life, you will not only feel how the person is feeling but also help the person.

It's a recipe for better relationships by putting all three together – Daniel Goleman

CHAPTER 3: HAPPINESS

The Hollywood actor Will Smith played the role of Chris Gardner in the movie *"The Pursuit of Happiness"*. The movie was based on a true story, and Chris struggled in his life over nearly one year looking for his happiness.

There was one quote that has been stuck in my head since I watched the movie. He says:

*"It was right then that I started thinking about Thomas Jefferson on the Declaration of Independence and the part about our right to life, liberty, and the pursuit of happiness. And I remember thinking how did he know to put the pursuit part in there? That maybe happiness is something that we can only pursue, and **maybe we can actually never have it**. No matter what. How did he know that?"*

Is the feeling of happiness temporary? Is it like the diminishing of marginal utility, where the second bite of food is less satisfying than the first? Is that why we can only pursue happiness and never be happy all the time? It seems there are more questions than answers.

Speaking of the pursuit of happiness, the first thing that comes to my mind is a class taught at Yale University. The class is the most popular class in over the 300 years of Yale history. It's called "Psychology and Good Life" taught by Dr. Santos. This chapter is a mix of the summary of that class and my own research.

43. Misconceptions

Here are statistics on happiness levels in your age group:

- 40.1% of college students report being so depressed "it's difficult to function"
- 53.1% of college students say they feel hopeless
- 61.4% of college students say they experience overwhelming anxiety
- 64.4% of college students report feeling lonely
- 86.9% of college students say they feel overwhelmed by all they have to do

Just looking at these statistics makes you depressed, doesn't it? Here is another one.

- In 1940s, the average happiness level was 7.5 out of 10. Now it's 7.2 out of 10

Today we have more clothes, shoes, TVs, cars, and gadgets compared to 80 years ago. There was no Facebook, Video Games, or Amazon with 2-day free shipping back then!! The average household income is certainly more, right? How are we not happier than we were in 1940?

It turns out that our minds' strongest intuitions are often wrong. Multiple studies show that most of the goals that we thought would make us happy didn't really make us happy. For example,

- Money
- Gadgets
- Love
- A perfect body

So, what does make us happy? Before we get there, let's talk about why our intuitions are wrong.

44. Our Minds Lie to Us about What Will Make Us Happy

In the field of Game Theory, there are things called finite and infinite games. Finite games have a known set of rules and a known set of participants. These participants agree upon objectives beforehand. For example, football or volleyball. The game ends when time runs out or when someone scores a certain number of points. Infinite games, on the other hand, have rules that change and may have unknown participants. The objective is to survive and to perpetuate the game. For example, running business or having relationships. There is no winning or losing in infinite games, but the participants can drop out due to lack of will or resources to continue.

The problem that most of us are having without realizing it, is that we seek our happiness in the context of a finite game. We think we'll be happy when we make $x per year or get a particular item. We think we'll be happy if we find true love or lose x lbs in 3 months.

Dr. Diener, aka "Dr. Happiness", is a leading researcher in positive psychology. Although emotional well-being rises with an increase in income until it reaches a certain amount, his study found that the correlation between money people made and happiness they felt was less than 0.1. (Correlation ranges from -1 to 1. If it's close to 0, two things are not correlated at all.) Furthermore, those who won lotteries were happy at the moment they won, but then their happiness level gradually normalized to where it was before they won the lottery. Sometimes they actually ended up less happy than before.

The same goes for Gadgets, love, a perfect body, and so on. Studies found that materialists had lower life satisfaction than non-materialists and had more mental health disorders. Lucas et al. found no support for the idea that happiness increases after marriage. Jackson et al. found those who lost weight improved well-being by reducing cardio-metabolic risk but found no evidence of psychological benefits. In fact, they found those who lost weight were more depressed than those who maintained or gained weight. Von Soest et al. found that body image actually worsened, and that suicidal ideation and use of alcohol increased for those who had cosmetic surgery.

Pursuit of happiness follows the concept of infinite games. There is no winning or losing. The objective is to perpetuate the good habits.

What are the good habits? The details are yet to come. First let's ask an important question.

"Can we ever become truly happy?"

The next section reveals some important facts that you may find interesting.

45. The Science of Happiness

Over the last few decades, scientists have been shifting their attention from "What's wrong with people?" to "What's good with people?", which is the basic concept of studying happiness. It turns out that there are three major parts that were responsible for one's happiness.

- Genetic (50%)
- Actions/thoughts (40%)
- Life Circumstances (10%)

Although we can't do much about genetics, an interesting thing is that life circumstances don't matter as much as we think. For example, the researchers found that the happiness levels for people who won the lottery were the same 3 months after winning as they were before winning. On the other hand, the happiness levels for those who experienced bad life events were the same 3 months after the event as they were before the misfortune.

The good news is that we can control 40% of our happiness based on our actions and thoughts. The bad news is that it takes effort and time.

Happiness does not simply happen. It must be prepared for and cultivated by each person, by setting challenges that are neither too demanding nor too simple for one's abilities
- Mihaly Csikszentmihalyi

What are practical things we have to do? Let's get back to the question in the previous section. What are the good habits? Here is the list of 7 habits of highly happy people

- Make time for Social Connections
- Limit time on Social Media: Good and Bad
- Help Others
- Give gratitude
- Exercise, Sleep, Meditate
- Be in the Moment
- Invest in Time

We'll dive into each more deeply in the following sections.

46. Make Time for Social Connections

Balance between work and personal time in life is an important factor for our happiness. Since we cover work in a different chapter, let's talk about your personal time.

Through time budgeting, you'll find at least 1/3 of a day can be allocated to your personal time, assuming 1/3 goes into sleep and the other 1/3 goes into work. How do you spend the personal time? Some people may be still in school, working on a higher-level degree. Some people may be social butterflies, meeting others at happy hours. Some people may work so much that they have very little personal time. There are many possibilities.

Here is an interesting study conducted by Diener and Seligman in 2002. The question they raised was "How do happy people spend their time?"

Daily activities (Scale: 1 - 10)	Happy	Unhappy
Time spent alone	4.4	5.8
Time spent with family, friends, or lover	5.1	3.6

This result may be a typical "Chicken or Egg" scenario. It's not certain whether people are unhappy because they spend time alone or whether they spend time alone because they are unhappy. Diener and Seligman concluded that social relationships are necessary but not sufficient for happiness, meaning that social relationships do not guarantee happiness, but you won't be very happy without them.

Here is another study regarding social connections. Epley and Schroeder conducted a study to see if making connections with strangers would change people's well-being. They created 3 groups and gave each a directive for the duration of the study.

1. Make connections with strangers
2. Stay alone more often
3. Do what you want

It turned out that people who made social connections with strangers were happier than those who stayed alone, (Group 3 is a control group). These results answer my question earlier. People become happier because they spend time with others, rather than spending time with others because they are happy. I can personally agree with these results since I always talk with people next to me on airplanes and I become happier in the end.

Social relationships do not guarantee happiness, but you won't be very happy without them.

Next, let's talk about social connections through social media. This is a bit depressing.

47. Good and Bad on Social Media

I often see people in restaurants using cell phones at their tables. There are very few conversations because they are too busy updating their social media or texting. I wouldn't be surprised if they are texting each other at the same table. When the food comes, they don't eat it right away. First, they text each other "Hey food is ready". Then they take a picture of the food, and a selfie with the food. After they post it on their social media, they eat the food while checking other people's comments on their posts.

Don't get me wrong. Social connections are certainly important to happiness. But that's only true if you spend quality time together, not through social media. In fact, if you type "Social media makes me" in a Google search bar, you'll see the following:

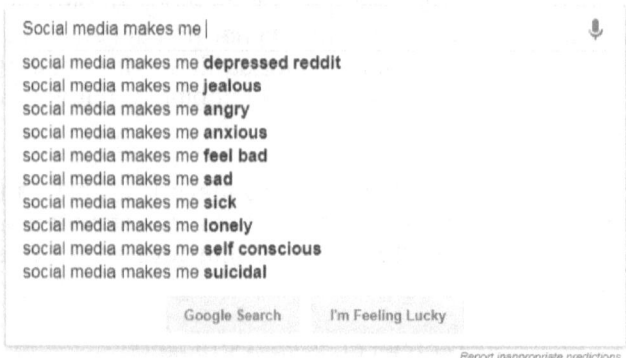

As if that weren't enough, social media use can open you up to cyberbullying and FOMO (Fear of Missing Out). Some people rank their friendships based on social media app-use frequency.

Don't get me wrong - social media can be good, too. It provides people with opportunities to speak up or to crowdfund social justice projects for national issues. You may also meet people online who later become friends in person.

In this modern society, we may not be able to live without social media no matter how good or bad it is. But listen to your heart and find out how it has been affecting you personally.

48. Help Others

Volunteerism is becoming very popular among larger companies. The employees spend their day or a half day helping the community with good causes. I've been involved on such occasions. In the end, I feel good about it.

Modern psychological research has shown that caring has benefits for all involved. People who volunteer or care for others tend to have better psychological well-being and higher life satisfaction. Those who receive social support are more protected from disease and death (Broadhead et al., 1983).

Here is an interesting study about one's happiness. Dunn et al. (2008) conducted an experiment, in which the researchers asked random people to rate their happiness, then gave them $20. The participants had a choice to spend the $20 on themselves or on others. After spending the money, the participants were asked about their happiness. It turned out that the happiness of those who spent the $20 on others is much greater than that of those who spent it on themselves. Also, the amount of money was not correlated with how happy the participants felt after they spent the money.

Helping others makes us happier than we expect!

Have you volunteered and helped people because you were intrinsically motivated? Have you volunteered because you truly believed in helping others, not for your resume or college applications?

It's not a bad thing that some students do a short-term volunteer activity for their resume. In the end, the outcome to the community is the same regardless of the motivation. The difference though, is that the happiness or satisfaction level is much higher among those who do it for the sake of volunteering than those who do it for other reasons. Intrinsic motivation beats Extrinsic motivation. (Midlarsky, Kahana, 1993).

What do these studies tell us? First, helping and caring for others is always beneficial for all involved. Second, if you can, spend your time or money to help others, rather than just yourself, for greater satisfaction. Just imagine how you feel when you spend your money to buy paint and spend your own personal time volunteering to paint houses for those who need support. Needless to say, imagine how people react when you tell them about that (not in a bragging way though).

49. Give Gratitude

Positive psychology is the scientific study of what makes life most worth living. The field is founded on the belief that people want to lead meaningful and fulfilling lives, to cultivate what is best within themselves, and to enhance their experiences of love, work, and play.

Of all the areas studied in the field of positive psychology, gratitude has been focused on and researched the most. According to the studies, grateful people have been shown to have greater positive emotion, a greater sense of belonging, and lower depression and stress.

What is recommended to create lasting positive change within yourself is to give gratitude 3 times every day for the next 3 weeks. After 3 weeks of the practice, the brain will start retaining the pattern of scanning the world for the positive. In other words, you will start seeing the world differently in a positive way.

I have a family friend who posts 3 things for which he is grateful to his family members on the kitchen wall every day. Since I've know them for a while, I can tell the changes in them before and after they started the practice. They now seem much happier and more positive in their attitudes than before.

Create ripples of positivity by giving gratitude.

Zappos, an on-line shoe and clothing retailer, is known for their service. Tony Hsieh, Zappos CEO, calls the company "the service company that happens to sell shoes". Not only do they send personalized thank-you notes to the customers, they also they send some thoughtful add-ons. For example, they sent a baby blanket to a customer who had a screaming infant in the background of a phone call. They sent Slip 'N Slide tickets to a family with four girls who needed something fun to do over the summer.

If you prefer keeping it to yourself, journaling and writing down a few things for which you are grateful is the easiest and most popular practice. Exposing yourself to the positive feelings by journaling can enhance empathy and self-esteem and reduce your stress.

My favorite practice is "Bedtime Thank-you" also known as "Count your Blessings". This, of course, can be done by yourself. I believe though, this is most effective if you practice it with your children. It helps your children to think of happy things that happened to them during their day and ensures they drift off to sleep with a heart full of gratitude.

50. E.S.M. – Exercise, Sleep, Meditate

Physical and mental conditions are both equally important in your pursuit of happiness. Without one or the other, it will be very difficult to continue your life the way you want to.

Exercise:
As you know, Exercise provides you with both physical and mental benefits. It's easy to measure the progress and success. It's easy to set goals and action plans. Researchers have shown that 30 minutes of cardio every day is as effective as 15mg of Zoloft, (an anti-depression medicine).

One of my co-workers who lost 200+ lbs once said, "At first, I wanted to walk to the mail box without becoming short of breath. Then I wanted to take the stairs. Then I wanted to do this and that. Next thing I knew, I had journeyed through a series of steps to get where I am now, losing 200+ lbs." She seems very happy having set and achieved goals. She enjoyed the process as much as the result.

Sleep:
Sleep is something we often take for granted. In fact, it is as important to life and health as the air we breathe. Doctors would recommend in general we sleep for about 7 ~ 8 hours each night. Sometimes it's more based on how busy your day is because sleep plays an important role in a number of processes, including memory consolidation and brain cleanup.

You know by now how poorly your body functions with too little sleep one night. Then, you get a venti iced caramel brulee latte with double shots of espresso, soy milk, and extra whipped cream and sprinkles from Starbucks to survive your day. Next thing you know, you are hooked on their coffee and can't start a day without caffeine! Does that sound familiar? Or you may see people in your office who carry a large tumbler with a lot of coffee every morning.

Meditation:

Science based benefits of meditation are that it...
- Reduces stress
- Controls anxiety
- Promotes emotional health
- Enhances self-awareness
- Lengthens attention span
- Makes you generally kinder
- Improves sleep
- Decreases blood pressure

If you want to treat yourself after a busy week, go to a gym, get a good meal, and massage while meditating, then end with a good night's sleep. You'll be much better off physically and mentally compared to staying up late partying.

51. Be in the Moment

As I mentioned in the Invisible wall section, a cell phone and lap top created an invisible wall between the father and his daughter. He unintentionally avoided making a social bond. She must have felt left alone, lonely, and sad because the wall indicated she wasn't his priority...
The real problem is that the violator usually does not feel guilty or does not realize how the other feel at the moment till the violator becomes the victim. I didn't feel guilty keeping my eyes on the screen or a cell phone when someone came by and asked me questions. When I visited others for help while they had their eyes on the screen or cell phones, I didn't feel that I was important to them. Since then, I make sure to turn my body to them, put my cell phone away and give 100% of my attention when they come and see me. The relationships with the co-workers have never been better than now because of that.

Multitasking is the biggest enemy of being in the moment

Here is another example. Some people tend to eat and read at the same time especially when alone. The more interesting the articles are, the less flavor they can taste because their brains focus on the article more. The problem is that they are not enjoying the meal, which can lead to unhealthy food choices, eating too quickly, and overeating.

Studies show that enjoyment tells the parasympathetic nervous system to trigger its relaxation response. This is the response that helps your digestion by relaxing the muscles and increasing digestive juices. Taste matters when it comes to nutrient absorption.

It is intriguing that some Buddhist practices of mindful eating involve giving students a few raisins and instructing them to take 10 or 20 minutes to eat them to truly experience the taste, smell, and sensation of every bite, and ultimately appreciate the food.

Being in the moment is a simple act of human behavior. It's the only method that allows you to truly enjoy and appreciate what you do. Time is limited. You might as well enjoy it.

52. Invest in Time

When you are in 20s, you may feel as though you have so much time left in your life. With that mind-set, it's easy to waste your time watching TV that doesn't truly interest you or updating your multiple social media accounts. What you don't realize is that you've already finished more than 25% of your life, assuming you'd live up to the average life expectancy of 80 years. That's scary, isn't it? Investing in time though, can help you have better quality and length of life.

Just like finance, investing in time yields returns. They can be high returns such as better memories and more meaningful experiences, or low returns such as dull and non-exciting days. Here are 3 investments in time that will help you live a longer, happier life

Invest in Life Extending Time

It's common sense to invest your time and energy taking care of your health, which yields you more time in the future. But we often take our health for granted by eating junk food, not exercising, or having bad habits till a doctor tells us the truth. Unfortunately, your metabolism won't be high forever. Investing your time creating healthy habits is worth every second. Otherwise, you'll be spending your time dealing with health problems in the future.

Invest in Problem-solving Time

One thing I hate is looking for something like a key or my cellphone. It can add up to many hours or even days looking for them throughout a life. That's just a waste. One day, I spent 20 minutes to set up a key holder at the entrance and a charging station in the kitchen. Now I know exactly where my stuff is every time so zero time is wasted. My 20 minute of time investment was definitely worth it.

Another example is if you spend hours sitting in a traffic every day, leave your house for work 2 hours early to avoid the traffic. You can work out before work and still get to the office before your normal time. That's two birds with one stone!

Invest in Cushion Time

Princeton University had a study in 1973, called the Good Samaritan Study, where the researchers put an injured person in front of people to see who would help. It turned out whether people were in a hurry or not impacted the results. Only 10% of those in a big hurry stopped and helped the injured. 45% of people in a medium hurry did so. But 63% of people who were not in a hurry stopped to help.

Creating cushion time will provide you with emotional leeway as well, which allows you to pay more attention to details. You'll make fewer mistakes and have more time to reevaluate what you do.

Also, if you happen to meet the mate of your dreams, but you meet them at a moment when you are in a big hurry, because you left yourself no cushion time, you might run right past them and never make that critical connection. Life rarely gives you the second chance. Take it or you lose it.

Time flies by whether you realize it or not. Next thing you know is that you'll be in your 30s and 40s. Spend your time wisely by investing it now for the future.

53. Love Won't Make You Happy

Love: strong affection for another arising out of kinship or personal ties. Attraction based on sexual desire, admiration, benevolence, or common interests.

What does it mean to love someone? Well, you know the feeling. When you're in love, you can't stop thinking about it, feeling like you are high, and trying to make your significant other happy. It sounds like love makes you happy, doesn't it?

One of the misconceptions our mind is telling us, is that Love makes us happy. In fact, it doesn't. If it did, then why do people get divorced?

Love does make you feel great though. it's associated with many positive feelings, at least in the short term. For example, love reduces stress. According to a study by the University of North Carolina, couples who hug regularly have less stress, improved mood, and lower blood pressure.

Another study shows that love can help you to live longer. A study from UCLA concluded that unmarried people have higher mortality rates because married couples positively influence each other's lifestyles.

The Japanese Character for Love is a combination of two words - <u>Heart</u> and <u>To Receive</u>

Love is not only about positive experiences. Love does bring on negative experiences as well because love is highly attention-seeking around uncertainty. Have you ever wondered whether your significant other loves you, if they'll ask to marry you, or whether they'll be The One? That anxiety and nervousness are also associated with love.

Love causes a mix of positive and negative experiences. Sometimes it makes you feel like you are on the top of the mountain and sometimes it makes you feel like you've hit rock bottom. Although love won't make you consistently happy, I'm not suggesting that you ignore it. Despite all the negatives such as uncertainty, broken promises, and misery, love is still worth having in your life.

Focus on your happiness using the previous sections in this chapter with your significant other. Positive feelings of love and strong relationships will follow and enrich your life.

54. To Be or Not to Be (Married)

People have started thinking differently about marriage in recent years. Marriage has become more about status than necessity. People used to think of marriage as a way to financial stability. Now college grads are less likely to think marriage should provide financial security since individuals can provide financial support for themselves. At the very least people defer their marriages until later. In 1960, 68% of 20 somethings were married, whereas only 26% in 2008.

Although the divorce rate has been dropping, experts estimate the chance of divorce is still roughly 40%.

As mentioned in the previous section, love is associated with many positive feelings, at least for a short term. Maybe that's why Linda Wolfe, who holds the record for being the most married woman in the world, got married 23 times.

Happy is the man who finds a true friend, and far happier is he who finds that true friend in his wife – Franz Schubert

Marriage is totally a personal choice. To me, the best 3 choices I made were getting Lasik surgery on my eyes, a Honda Odyssey (I love my mini-van) and married. I think of my marriage as not only financial security but also filling in what I'm missing. I can only see 180 degrees of vision, and if she can see the other 180 degrees, we are complete. The first year of marriage was certainly the hardest. We ate burnt suppers the whole year, got upset and angry more often, and almost gave up on it. I threw towels many times, but she picked them up and said, "Let's try again". She is certainly my better half. She makes me realize, despite the many emotional roller-coaster rides, that I smile more often and see the world more colorfully.

That being said, my vote goes to "Yes" on marriage. At least for now.

How did she and I ever get married? Well, I'm pleased to tell you that after years and years of asking, and asking, and asking...

I finally said yes.

55. Flow

Positive psychology can't be mentioned without Flow. What is flow?

Flow is the feeling you experience when you are in the zone or get completely lost in something you love. It's the mental state of operation in which you are fully immersed in a feeling of energized focus, focused on performing an activity such as cooking, writing, painting, or running. The concept was named by Mihaly Csikszentmihalyi, one of the world's leading researcher on positive psychology, in 1975.

When you are in the flow state, you create the perfect space to find yourself. Furthermore, you lose all sense of time and space.

For example, artists, especially painters, get so immersed in their work that they forget they are hungry, thirsty, or even sleepy.

Flow is also studied in the field of sport psychology as athletic performance is much higher when they are in the zone.

Lyoto Machida, a former Ultimate Fighting Championship Light Heavyweight Champion, uses meditation techniques before fights to attain Mushin, an empty mind, a concept similar to flow.

Gandhi also described the flow state of mind.

The best way to find yourself is to lose yourself in the service of others – Mahatma Gandhi

Not only athletics or arts, but also religion and spirituality have concepts similar to flow. For example, Japanese Zen Buddhism uses these concepts to aid their mastery of disciplines.

Flow is used in many disciplines. It's almost required to perform at the highest level or to master any discipline. The question is how to get into the zone? These are the required conditions.

- Goals are clear
- Feedback is immediate
- A balance between opportunity and capacity is reasonable

Flow has a positive effect on one's life. People who experience flow seem to have intense feelings of enjoyment, which will lead to happiness in the long run.

56. Awe

Have you experienced that a cup of coffee tasted better, ordinary buildings or streets looked more fascinating, or people seemed nicer during holidays or on vacation? I remember the best croissant I ever had was from a small convenience store at a train station in France. It was not from some 3-star restaurant or well-known bakery. I was on a vacation, excited about everything, in France, and having "Awe" moments. This croissant from an ordinary convenience store made my vacation worth going.

There is something about this Awe moment that gives us a sense of pleasure and excitement in our lives. This is another reason why many people travel to big cities during holiday seasons to look at the decorations throughout the towns.

How about when you are admiring great art, visiting the Grand Canyon, or seeing amazing scenes under the water? We have this moment of Awe too, don't we?

Although not many studies have been done on the Awe moment, many of us know the feeling, which diminishes our sense of self-importance and creates a small-self perspective. In other words, the Awe experience makes you realize you are a small piece of this great world.

One study at the University of California at Berkeley shows that the feeling of small-self in Awe moments leads to better social relationships, which ultimately leads to a sense of happiness and well-being.

The question is "Do we have to travel the world or go to different museums to feel Awe?" Well, hopefully not. Try to bring this same feeling to your everyday life by changing the way you look at things. For example, Polaris, also known as the North Star, is about 680 light years away. That means it takes light 680 years to travel from the star to Earth. In other words, the light you are seeing right now is about 680 years old!!

Feel the Awe!

57. Accept

Do you know The Greek myth of Icarus? Icarus was the son of Daedalus, a craftsman, Daedalus creates a pair of wings with wax and feathers so that they can escape from an island. Daedalus warns Icarus not to fly too high or too low. Icarus, in spite of the warning, flies too high, too close to the sun, which causes the wax to melt. He falls to his death.

One of the lessons you can learn from the myth is not to make yourself into more than you are. To put it simply - Accept your limits! Icarus might have been able to escape from the island if he had stayed within the altitude limits his father dictated.

Many people tend to ignore their limits, meaning they do not accept the facts. For example, Japanese high school seniors give up one or more years by studying if they don't get into the college of their choice. One year might be worth sacrificing if the college provides you with paths to your dream job. If you fail two years in a row though, maybe that's not the path you should be pursuing. I personally know someone with 4 attempts. By the time he entered college, his high school friends were graduating. My opinion was that he should've accepted his limit and looked for other options to leverage his strengths instead.

The intensity of our pain depends on our level of resistance to the present moment – Eckhart Tolle

When you accept your limits and the present moment, you'll feel the inner peace and you can pour more energy into other things within your control. Icarus and Daedalus could have accepted that humans couldn't fly with just wings and poured their energy into the development of air planes.

This can be applied to many events in life such as break-ups in relationships, lay-offs at work, deaths, and so on. Accept the present moment and move on!

58. Too Many Options Make People Miserable

Many of us believe that the more options we have, the more freedom we'll get, and that freedom is a key to living a happier life. Unfortunately, this is another misconception that your brain is telling you. The truth is, many options will make people miserable.

We are living in a society where we have so many options given, from a cup of coffee to college degrees. Starbucks, for example, claims to have 80,000 different options to choose from. That'll take roughly 220 years to try them all if you try one cup of different coffee from Starbucks every day.

Studies found three reasons why many options make people miserable.

Many options paralyze people: when I go to a Starbucks and I'm staring at the menu, I look like a deer in the headlights. I freeze because I have too many options to choose from. After staring at that menu for 10 minutes and letting a few people pass me, I usually end up with a small coffee.

- Many options raise one's expectations: when you see many options, your brain tends to think there must be good ones there. Even if your choice is good, you do not get as much satisfaction because of the high expectations. Furthermore, in the back of your head, you tend to think there may be a better option than what you have, an option that you're missing (FOMO – Fear Of Missing Out). If there are only a few options, your expectations may be lower and easier to meet. You also will have less FOMO.

- Many options cause self-blame: There is no one but you to blame when the option you choose fails. On the other hand, if there is only one option to choose and the option is bad, you cannot be blamed.

- For example, when a family member is on a life support, a doctor gives two options;
    1. Keep the life support but the person might not survive. Even he survives, he may be a vegetable for the rest of his life.
    2. Stop the life support and he'll die in a few hours.
    Almost all families choose option 2. Years later, they feel negative about the experience.

On the other hand, when a doctor does not give options, meaning the families are told the life support must be stopped, the families feel positive about the experience years later.

Clinical depression has exploded in the industrial world, around the same time we started seeing more options in life.

The days when we had to choose only the size of a cup in ordering a coffee are gone. Although we will see more and more options in the future, we should know many options make people miserable. One way to avoid this is to let someone else decide for you. The families from the previous example could let the doctor decide even though the options were given.

Just like anything else, anything too extreme can be problematic. Letting others decide everything for you is another problem. In the Self-Improvement chapter, I'll talk about Decision Making.

59. Synthetic Happiness

Over a 15-year period, I always wanted a pickup truck. After getting a stable job and a financial cushion, I thought I was able to get it. Then, it became a mini-van.

Unfortunately, most of us don't always get what we want. It's a fact in life. When our expectations in life don't match with the reality, we get disappointed and unhappy...

However, it turns out that I LOVE my mini-van. I am as happy as I would be with a pickup truck. Why is that?

The answer is Synthetic Happiness. Researches show that our ability to cope with unfavorable situations is greater than we think. Synthetic happiness is a system of cognitive processes that help us change our views of the world. In other words, you can create your own happiness within yourself.

Dan Gilbert, author of Stumbling on Happiness, is the leading researcher of Synthetic happiness. He calls it a mental immune system. He says, "The psychological immune system works best when we are totally stuck, when we are trapped. This is the difference between dating and marriage. You go out on a date with a guy, and he picks his nose; you don't go out on another date. You are married to a guy and he picks his nose. He has a heart of gold, but don't touch the fruitcake!"

In dating, you look to get what you want. In marriage, you find a way to like what you've got – Dan Gilbert

When you are given options, you tend to think about the outcomes of the other choices you don't pick, which causes you to be less happy. On the other hand, when you are not given options, you tend to look at what you have and its bright sides.

Here are some interesting statistics. Global Divorce Rate for Love Marriage is 55% whereas for Arranged Marriage is 6%.

Although some of the success is due to the cultural differences, people who choose their own spouse are more likely to seek divorce, hoping to find a better spouse rather than fixing it.

It's not a denial but looking at a bright side of what you have. I didn't have any options but a mini-van, but I ended up liking it because I changed the view on the mini-van. Synthetic happiness can help you look at bright sides of what you have and manufacture happiness within yourself.

CHAPTER 4: FINANCE

As I mentioned it in the previous chapter, Money will not make you truly happy. That's why Lottery winners are not happier afterwards. In fact, the more money we come across the more problems we see.

It's also true that it's nice not to worry obsessively about your finance, either. The most important thing here is to change your mind-set. Your personal finance is an infinite game. There is no winning or losing. The object is to survive (especially, to survive when you can't work or produce any more income). Your retirement fund will become very important to you eventually. You are either looking for your first job or recently got a job. Ironically, you already have to think about your retirement. We'll talk about that in this chapter.

Your monthly budgeting and management of your cash flow, and assets and liabilities are top topics in this chapter, which will save you some $ to offset what you paid for this book and gain more. You might be able to save half a million dollars! (I'm not kidding) I'll show you that later.

60. The Richest Time of Your Life

If you are a recent college grad in your early 20s, the chance of having roommates and sharing utility bills with others is high, which means your expenses are very little, which makes this the richest time of your life, though you may not be making much money because it's not how much you are making but it's how much left after all the expenses.

I remember that I was able to afford $20 to $25 bottles of wine in my mid-20s, low $10 bottles in my early 30s after I got married, and $4 bottles of wine (thanks to Trader Joes) in my mid-30s after my children were born. My salary is definitely higher now than in my 20s, but I feel as though I have less money because of higher expenses. By the way, kids are expensive… in case you didn't know.

This information certainly does not apply to all, but it's good information to have since you need to do something about the excess of money in your early or mid-20s. Here is one good tip for you.

Do Not Save Money.

This advice does apply to all including me. I currently do not save money, but I do something else. I'll get to it in later section in this chapter. Meanwhile, here is a list of contents in this chapter.

Budget
Tax
Invest
Bank Accounts
Credit Cards

61. Financial Rules of Thumb

There isn't one rule that applies to everyone. However, these rules of thumb are good guidelines for real world freshmen like you. Here I'll show you a number of financial Rules of Thumb.

50/30/20 Rule:
50% of your income should go toward necessities such as housing and bills
30% of your income should go toward your entertainment
20% of your income should go towards financial goals such as investments

This is a good starting point if you haven't done this before. Although these proportions will change over time based on your needs, try to keep at least 20% towards financial goals.

300/20 Rule:
Find a house that costs less than 300% of your gross income and be sure to put 20% down.

For example, if your annual salary is $60k, find a house less than $180k. With 20% down, you will not have to pay mortgage insurance.

6-months Emergency Fund Rule:
Have 6-months' worth of savings on hand in case of an emergency.

I used to believe in that. As I was doing research on this chapter, I found an interesting article. Based on that, I suggest you save $0 in the savings, and I'll explain why in a later section

Age Rule for Stocks:
Since Stocks can be risky, you want to invest in stocks in your early days but not as much in later years. Subtract your age from 120. That is the percentage that you should be investing in stocks at that age.

For example, in your 20s, invest 90+% of your money into stocks. As you grow older, invest more into less risky securities such as bonds.

20/4/10 Rule:
When buying a car, you should put down at least 20%, finance it for less than 4 years, and spend less than 10% of your gross income on transportation costs

For example, if your annual salary is $60k, less than $6,000 should go towards transportation costs, which includes loan payments, gas, maintenance, and insurance. Let's assume the annual costs for gas, maintenance, insurance, and loan interest are $600, $400, $1,200 and 4%, respectively. Then your annual loan payment will be $3,800 for 4 years, which allows you to spend $17,000 on a car with a 20% down payment. Sorry, you won't be buying a Tesla for a while.

62. Take Advantage of Tax Benefits and Have Multiple Financial Options

Disclaimer: I'm not a CPA or financial advisor. Therefore, please consult with a professional or do research, and never make decisions based on this section without any due diligence.

The IRS created a set of rules to indicate how much taxes you should pay when you make income. It also created a set of rules for us to reduce taxable income. I'll cover the tip of the iceberg. Be sure to know sufficient tax information so that you get as much benefit as possible and don't cheat on the system.

There are multiple types of retirement plans such as Roth IRA, 401(k), 403(b), 457 plans, Simple IRA plans, SEP plans... etc. Please check the types of retirement plans at the IRS website for the most updated information.

Depending on employers, you might have a benefit of Company Matching, which means the companies will put free money into your retirement fund up to a certain percentage. Make sure to max it out. Also, if possible, do not take the money out of the fund till you retire. Otherwise, you may have to pay a penalty for early withdraw.

There are many retired people who rely on only social security because the social security looked reasonable and sufficient while they were working. Unfortunately, they never put their money into other retirement vehicles. As a result, some of them are struggling now.

Financial advisors will show you how much money you should put into retirement every month, which makes you feel safe for your future. I do respect their knowledge and expertise, but the truth is that no one can predict what the world will be like in 40 years.

Remember those who are struggling now, relying on only social security, felt safe about their future when they were at your age, too!!

Another recession might occur, your portfolio might not perform as well as expected, or machines might take over the world, (you never know). My point is not to put all of your eggs in one basket. Have multiple financial plans just in case. I'll cover that in the next section

63. Financial Tips

Assets/Liabilities
Robert Kiyosaki, the author of *Rich Dad Poor Dad*, gives a good piece of advice in his book. He defines Asset and liability differently. In his book,
> Asset: something that will increase your money
> Liability: something that will decrease your money

For example, securities such as bonds and stocks are assets because they increase their values over time. Meanwhile, car is a liability because its value is decreasing over time.

Here is a good question. How about your money in the savings accounts?

Money in a savings account is an asset if we apply the general definition of Asset. It also increases over time because of interest that the bank agrees to pay. However, it's a liability according to his definition since inflation within the economy is greater than the interest rate. In the end, the money is losing value over time. Therefore, every time you put more money into a savings account, it's like taking 3 steps forward and 2 steps back... this is the reason I invest money rather than save it.

Allocate your money into multiple assets over time.

It's safer to have multiple small incomes rather than one big income during your retirement.

Student Loan
There is no doubt that loans are liabilities. They are the holes in your wallet. They might become negotiable by declaring bankruptcy, but the penalty can be severe.

Student loan, unfortunately, will stay with you forever, meaning you can't declare bankruptcy on it. Take care of that sooner than later.

Learn to cook
Obviously, there are multiple benefits from this. You definitely save a lot of money if you bring lunch to work. Studies show your overall health is better if you fix your meals. Additionally, your partner will appreciate you if you can cook!

Call for discount
Every dollar matters! When a promotion period is about end, call their customer centers and ask if any offers are available. Truth is they can do more than you think. Sometimes good deals are not listed on-line. The only way to find out is to call and ask for it.

64. Don't Save Money

Let's go back to the statement from earlier. Why shouldn't we save money? For those who have taken Financial mathematics in college, this is obvious. If not, let's talk about it for a minute.

Assume Bank A offers 0.5% interest in their savings account, and the average rate of inflation in the economy is 3%. $100 in the savings account in one year will be $100.5. Discount the value back to present by dividing it by 1.03, which is equal to $97.57 (-$2.43). In just one year, you lose $2.43 by leaving it in the savings account. In 10 years, you lose over 20% of the original value.

Keeping it as cash is even worse since you don't get the 0.5% of interest that Bank A offers. The solution is easier than you think. Invest instead of saving.

Let's compare two scenarios. Scenario A is to put $100 into a savings account monthly that gives 1% interest annually. Scenario B is to invest $100 monthly into mutual funds that gives an average of 8% return. In 30 years, Scenario A has the balance of $42,000 whereas Scenario B has $150,000. It sounds too good to be true, doesn't it?

Truth is, you may have never invested your money before. No worries. You can start with very little money. Also, investing is something you learn as you go. Or simply talk to someone you trust.

Here is a list of things people wish they have done when they were your age.

Answers	
Invest	30%
Relax. Take vacations. Rest	16%
Go back to school	9%
Work hard	9%
Be on time	5%
Learn something new every day	5%
Change the job if you don't like it	5%
Budget	4%
Others	17%

If you don't start investing your money now, at some point in your life you will. Then you will wish you would have done it early.

Investment comes in many shapes, sizes, and colors. It can be Stocks, Bonds, Mutual Funds, Foreign Exchange, Real Estate, Energy, Person-to-Person Loan, Gold... and so on. There is always one or more for everyone.

Please keep a few things in mind. There is always a risk associated with investing. In general, high risk = high return. You can always mitigate the risk by diversifying, meaning to allocating eggs into multiple baskets, not one. Also, investment is a long-term strategy. Remember that Rome wasn't built in a day.

65. Investments

In the previous section, Scenario B had 8% of return. Where is 8% coming from?

Here is the graph of annual average Market Returns over 140 years. The average is roughly 12% *[1]. Even excluding outliers such as -40% or 60%, the average would be still higher than 8%, which means Scenario B is still conservative.

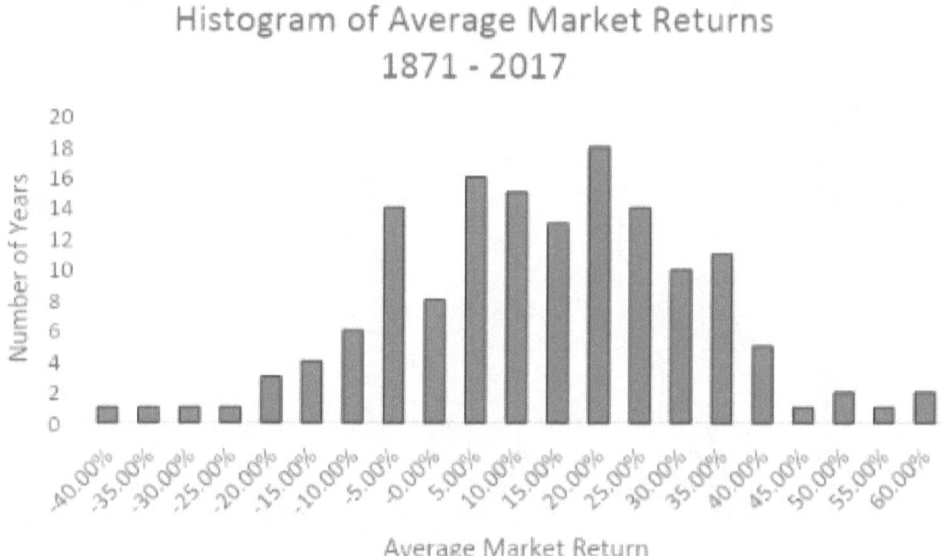

Most of us, including me, have a tough time tracking every single stock or mutual fund that is traded in the US. But there's no reason to worry - we have good news. Some experts have done their homework for us by creating an Index, a smaller sample of the market that is representative of the whole. Investing in indices is a great way to start for beginners since it diversifies your portfolio automatically and mitigates its risk.

Another investment that suits beginners is Crowdfunding. There are a few primary types of crowdfunding investments
    Equity Investments: Investing in a company
    Real Estate Investments: Investing in property
    Peer to Peer Lending: Loaning money to others
    Specialty Investments: Investing in even more alternative ways

The reason why I think it's for beginners is the concept is straightforward. You know what return you'll get, how long your money is invested, and how much is charged in fees. It's as passive as it can be, so long as you do your due diligence. I've been doing Real Estate Crowdfunding and have no issues with it. The return is around 7 to 8% annually.

I can choose how long to invest it, too. It goes from 3 months to 20+ months. The fee is very reasonable. But again - Do your due diligence before any investments!

[1] Although a basic average return is not the same as an annualized average return, I'm keeping this math as simple as possible since exact math calculation is not important here. For more information regarding Market Returns, please google search the words.

66. Open Multiple Checking Accounts

Budgeting your money and managing your cash flows are "MUST KNOW" skills in your life. The problem is it's not easy for everyone. Some people like apps such as Mint or Albert that help them manage their money whereas others don't because they don't want to share their bank accounts with third parties, (which is understandable).

In this section, I'll share an idea that is easy to implement and very useful for managing your cash flow.

Most of you, assuming you are in your early 20s, have one bank account. Your employer pays you a salary into the account. Then, you pay bills, credit cards and entertainment expenses from the account. Well, so did I till a friend of mine shared her idea.

The problem of having only one account is that the more money you see the more money you tend to spend. Especially, when you have very little expenses, your account grows quicker. Next thing you know, you let your guard down and end up buying things you don't really need… Has it ever happened to you before?

The key is to create another checking account and call it Monthly Expenses. Then add up all your fixed monthly expenses such as mortgage or rent, car loan, insurance, gym membership fee, utilities (it's not fixed but it should be roughly the same every month) … etc. and move the amount into the Monthly Expenses account as soon as you get paid. If you are using the 50/30/20 rule, remove the 20% from your main checking account, too. What's left in your main checking account after all the transactions is your monthly allowance, much less than you are used to see. (Hopefully it's not negative.)

The beauty of having multiple accounts is that you can set up automatic payments for your expenses from the new account and you do not have to worry about whether you have enough money to pay them off each month.

With a Monthly Expenses account, you have one less thing to worry about. Good for you! Now you got 98 problems and she ain't one.

This simple yet powerful cash flow management tool will work for you for a long time. This is one of the things I wish I have known earlier since I could have saved a lot of money and time.

Do I use the tool now? The answer is - Not anymore. Once you purchase a house and build equity, you'll have another option to manage your cash flow and pay off your mortgage quicker. I'll cover the method in a later section, which may not apply to you yet in your life till all conditions are met such as owning a house and building equity.

67. Monthly Expenses Account

Let's dig a little deeper into what should be considered monthly expenses. As I mentioned in the previous section, you can think of mortgage or rent, Car loan, insurance, gym membership fee, utilities and so on. Anything that's fixed or nearly fixed and happens at a regular interval.

There are a few more items that you might want to include into the category. They are annual or semi-annual expenses, but you can easily convert them into monthly by dividing the approximate amounts by 12 or 6.

Holiday Fund
Statistics shows that people have been spending more on holiday gifts every year since 2008 except for 2012. According to the study, the average amount that US Adult spent during 2018 holiday season was $885. It will be nice if you can survive that time of a year without using your emergency fund or opening a new credit card that gives you 0% APR for a year and pay it off monthly.

Find out roughly how much you spent in the last three years and estimate the cost of the next holiday season. Divide it by 12 and start putting that amount into your Monthly Expense Account monthly.

Insurance
Some insurance companies give you an option to pay the premiums by monthly, semi-annually, or annually. For example, I pay my car insurance semi-annually. As you may know, it's cheaper to pay for a longer term. Just like the holiday expenses, it can make a big hole in your wallet.

Fortunately, the insurance premium is easier to estimate than Holiday Expenses. Calculate the monthly portion of an annual/semi-annual premium and start putting it into your Monthly Expense Account.

Some items shouldn't be considered as monthly expenses. For them, use the following methods to help you reduce expenses

Cash Budget
Sometimes we are not disciplined enough to limit our daily spending such as lunch or morning coffee. For certain items, I recommend using only cash. Take out only $20 or so weekly and use the cash for those items. Once it's gone, IT'S GONE.

Choose certain credit cards for particular purchases
Some credit cards give 3% cash back or points for Gas, groceries, or restaurants. You might want to shop around and find what's the best card you want to carry daily. The downside is that it's easy to over spend using credit cards. Be careful.

I'll cover more details on Credit cards in the next section.

68. Pros and Cons on Credit Cards

Let's cover the easy one - cons of credit cards. First, it is easy to over-spend your money since you delay the payments, and the credit limit can be high. Secondly, it can get stolen and be used to purchase large items that you are not aware of. Frequently checking your balance is important. Although all the fraudulent purchases will be reimbursed, it's a pain to call the credit card company, cancel the card, and activate a new one. Needless to say, you'll have to update any pre-set transactions from the old card such as Apple Pay or your gym membership fee.

Despite of all the cons, I believe it's still worth having credit cards because of their benefits.

Build Your Credit Score
This is the most obvious reason to hold credit cards. Your interest rates will depend on it when you borrow money from institutions such as mortgage or car loans. It's one way to prove that you're trustworthy. A 1% difference in interest rate can save you tens and even thousands of dollars.

Earn Rewards
Not only can you get either cash back or reward points when you use credit cards but also you get sign-up bonuses. One sign-up bonus was so good that I was able to travel oversea for free by signing up. Additionally, it gave me free access to a lounge in the airport and no foreign transaction fees.

Keep your eyes on the deals that credit card companies provide since great benefits are temporary.

Warranty and Insurance
Items you purchase using credit cards may have an extra warranty that you can take advantage of. Rental cars paid using credit cards may have extra insurance as well. Please see the details on the credit card you hold.

Some benefits are self-explanatory such as
0% Interest for 12 to 15 months
More purchasing options over the phone or via the internet
Convenient to carry

69. HELOC

It stands for Home Equity Loan of Credit, which is basically a loan against your house (in general up to 80% of your property value*1). For example, assume your house is worth $200,000, and you still owe $130,000. Then you can borrow up to $30,000 using the house as a collateral.

Just like credit cards, you pay interest on the loan once you use it. The beauty is that the rate is much less than any credit cards since your house is the collateral. Plus, you don't pay interest till you use it.

Why is this useful to you in the future? How will this help paying off the mortgage quicker?

Remember that there are certain conditions which have to be met first, which are 1. You own a property. 2. Loan to Value is less than 80%, and 3. You have savings.

Let's use the same example; the house is worth $200,000 and the mortgage balance is $130,000 (roughly you are in the 10th year of 30-year loan. See the loan schedule*2 below). Because you are a believer in the 6-month Emergency Fund, you have $35,000 in your savings account.

What if you pay off your mortgage partially with the Emergency Fund? Your balance is $95,000 in the 10th year rather than $130,000. Suddenly, you cut off your loan schedule by 7 years!! Not only that, in 30 years, I save you $90,000!!

Loan Schedule	Mortgage Balance	No Emergency Fund
1	$ 157,592	$ 157,592
2	$ 155,063	$ 155,063
3	$ 152,408	$ 152,408
...	...	...
9	$ 133,446	$ 133,446
10	$ 129,710	$ 94,710
...	...	...
22	$ 67,271	$ 4,416
23	$ 60,226	$ -5,772
...	...	...
28	$ 19,353	$ -64,879
29	$ 9,913	$ -78,531
30	$ 0	$ -92,865

You may question what if you need to use the emergency fund. That is when your HELOC comes into play. Remember you only pay interest if you use it. You can do the exact the same using your credit cards. The problem of using credit cards as emergency is the interest rates are much higher.

I'm highly against having any money in the savings account since it loses value over time from inflation. You might as well use it to pay off your mortgage partially, which ultimately saves you money.

*[1]Please contact banks for more details. The rates and actual amount you can borrow depend on the loan institutions
*[2]Loan schedule is based on 30-year fixed of 5% APR with 20% of down payment (See appendix 1)

70. Life Insurance

Do you need life insurance?

The answer is not easy since it depends on your situation. The main factors are 1. whether you have any loans or not and 2. whether you have a family. If the two answers are no, you probably don't need Life Insurance for now.

Factor 1: Loans
Federal student loans, which rarely require co-signs, are discharged when the borrower dies. In that case, you'll be fine without life insurance. If you have loans from private lenders with co-signers, make sure your life insurance will cover the amount. Otherwise, the co-signers will have to come up with cash to pay off your loans.

What if you are the co-signer? Some private student loans have conditions that go into automatic default when the co-signer dies, meaning the balance will be due immediately after you die. Yes, you'll need life insurance.

Factor 2: Family
If you have any kids, you already know they are EXPENSIVE! From my experience, it cost me $100 on formula and diapers every week per kid! Don't forget about Day care. I love them very much, but they almost made me go bankrupt.

There are a few different types of life insurance such as Whole life, Universal Life and Term life. In general, you will be just fine with a term life insurance for the following reasons.

- The cost is reasonable (Whole life can cost 4 times more than term)
- The market does not impact the insurance amount
- It gives what your family needs

CBS News had an article of how much it costs to raise a child. According to the article, the estimated cost of raising a child from birth through age 17 is $233,610. That's not counting prenatal care, childbirth or college tuition!!

If your answers to the two factors are both Yes, then amount of your insurance will be the sum of the two; you'll need to consider the loan amount as well as the cost to raise a child.

CHAPTER 5: COMMUNICATION

What is the most important skill to become successful?
- A. Critical Thinking
- B. Problem-solving
- C. Collaboration
- D. Creativity and innovation
- E. Communication
- F. Soft skills
- G. Technology

Obviously, they are all important in any organizations. However, if you think about this carefully, there is one thing in common among the options; Communication.

Critical thinkers need to be able to deliver their thoughts. Defining problems correctly and sharing the solutions requires high level communication skills. You can't collaborate without effective communication skills. Creative and innovative ideas can only be heard with a well-organized presentation. It goes on and on for the rest of the options.

That makes Communication the most important skill to have.

71. It's You

Speaking of something in common, I have a question for you. What is one thing all of your failed relationships have in common?

*It's **you**.*

This answer changes the way you see relationships, doesn't it? When I accepted that fact, I had to think why they failed, because maybe the answer was within myself. I realized that most of the arguments and conflicts were caused by misunderstanding and failing to communicate with each other. The results of my inability to communicate effectively with them are... well you already know.

Do you listen actively and speak effectively? Life will be much easier if we can do so in every conversation. Just like anything else, this skill takes a lot of practice.

In this chapter, I'll cover the Tips in communication.

72. Communication Styles

You might notice how your communication style changes depending on whom you talk to. Some people prefer getting to a point quickly, and others like to socialize more. It is important to recognize which communication style the person you are talking with prefers. There are four Communication styles.

Direct:
Direct communicators prefer when you get to the point quickly and in a succinct manner. When dealing with these communicators, be specific and avoid over-explaining or repeating yourself. Focus on solutions and only provide details when asked.

Initiating:
Initiating communicators value interacting with others and sharing stories. Allow time for socializing at the beginning of meetings and create a friendly, and non-threatening environment. Provide time for them to express their feelings and opinions.

Supportive:
Supportive communicators appreciate a calm, steady approach. Earn their trust by providing them with plenty of reassurance. When seeking their opinions and ideas, encourage them to express their concerns and allow them time to make decisions.

Analytical:
Analytical communicators like facts and figures. Present information to them in an organized manner and be prepared to answer questions. Be patient while they think through and process new information.

A good conversation is like a miniskirt - short enough to retain interest, but long enough to cover the subject.

Knowing the other person's preferred communication style can lead to higher efficiency and good morale, which increases satisfaction in personal and familial relationships.

Reference: Toastmasters International: Understanding Your Communication Style

73. Listen Actively

If you want to become an effective communicator, become a good listener.

The easiest way to improve your communication skill is to listen actively, which is very tiring because It takes more energy to listen than speak. Just to be clear, I'm not talking about just "hearing" but actively listening.

Many people fail to do so without noticing it. Active listening requires your 100% attention to understand the speakers. Often when people listen, their intention is to reply instead of to understand. They jump in with questions or comments before the speaker ends his conversation.

Here are 4 steps to become an active listener.

Turn your body to the speaker to show you are 100% engaged with them:
Body language speaks more than words. It's easy to tell whether the listeners are actively listening or not. Be in the moment.

Respond appropriately to what the speaker is saying:
Smile if the story is fun. Laugh if it's funny. Look sorry if it's sad.

Be patient. Don't jump in with questions and comments till the speaker finishes:
Speakers don't like to be interrupted. Let them finish their talk first before you take your turn.

Summarize what you hear to validate your understanding:
This is my favorite technique to show both that I'm listening actively and that I understand the message. It's dangerous to make any comments or suggestions without this step.

To effectively communicate, we must realize that we are all different in the way we perceive the world, and use this understanding as a guide to our communication with others
— Tony Robbins

Active listening increases the chance of having a good conversation with anybody. Try the steps above, and you'll see the impact of the active listening on your next communication.

74. Good Communication Fulfills a Woman's Primary Love Need

Here are a few tips that can be applied to the communication in your relationship.

Active Listening
I was guilty of not doing this. I used to get frustrated or angry in communicating with my wife and my previous relationships because I tended to listen in order to respond, rather than to understand what they said. Some men might recognize a similar situation in your past.

After learning to actively listen, I only focus on seeing the world through their eyes. I don't think about how to respond or think about what solutions to provide. All I do is to listen and rephrase what they say so that they know I understand their concerns correctly. Relationships have become easier (not easy) since then.

"I" sentence
Another communication skill that will help your relationship is to use "I" sentences in asking for favors. For example, if you want the trash to be taken outside, say "I'll be happy if you throw the trash away" instead of "Please, take the trash away... I said please!". It sounds much softer.

Will you? vs Can you? (Would you? vs Could you?)
I remember that the phrase "Can you?" used to bother me in my early years in the US when someone asked me a favor. The phrase "Can you?" meant "Are you physically able to?" to me at first. Of course, I could, most of the time. it's like the previous example, I was physically able to take the trash out when someone said, "Could you take the trash out?"

Did I want to? Probably not. Although I did it every time anyways, as a favor, I felt something was bugging me. Have you felt that before?

Others use "Will you?" or "Would you?". To me personally, this sounds better. There's nothing that bugs me about it.

Am I thinking too hard about this?

75. How to Persuade Others

One of the useful skills in effective communication is the power to persuade others. For example, Sales people are excellent at using this skill to convince others to buy their products. Dr. Martin Luther King used the "I have a dream" speech to start a civil movement. Aristotle, the famed Greek philosopher in the 4th century B.C., created the foundational concepts to persuade his disciples.

There are three areas you need to focus on in writing your speech to make it sound persuasive.

Ethics: Credibility is important. You have to get your audience to trust you.

Logic: Explain in clear and concise terms. Use comprehensive research to support your points.

Confusion can ruin your efforts easily when your points aren't clear. For example,

"In order to stop global warming, we should eat more vegetables".

It might be true. But it's hard to understand the connection unless you provide powerful evidence.

Emotion: Use storytelling to make your points more effective.

Once you get all the three areas embedded into your speech, the next step is to know your audience and to make sure it's appropriate. I don't think Dr. King's speech would have been effective or impactful to middle school students. Make sure to know whom you are speaking to!

After you prepare a speech that contains the three areas and you know your audience, it's time to persuade people. There are three steps you want to take during your speech to influence the thinking of others.

> Step1: Inspire – get the audience excited about your points.
> Step2: Convince – allow the audience to get on the same page.
> Step3: Call to action – give a clear and detailed action to take.

It takes time to persuade men to do even what is for their own good – Thomas Jefferson

76. Humor

There is not secret about it. People love Humor in a conversation or speech. It builds rapport and makes the distance between you and the listeners much shorter. It's a skill that can be relied on in any situations. Do you have to be funny to make others laugh? Not necessarily. I'll describe a few techniques below.

Laugh dominos: laughing is contagious. It spreads out like a flu. If you want the listeners to laugh, you laugh first.

Surprise: what triggers laughing is unexpected results. Misdirecting the listeners to assume a result is A but then you say B instead. For example, I went to a stadium for a live concert in Jacksonville FL. It turned out the concert was in Jacksonville, NC.

Embarrassment: share an embarrassing story, something from your own past. There's nothing more disarming and yet inspiring than someone who can chuckle at their past self. This psychological laughter trigger is a good way to provide comfort to the listeners, which makes the listeners think you are one of them.

Superiority: tell a story where you were in a tough spot. This makes the listeners feel superior and say "Thank God, it's not me". This can trigger a laugh at you by depreciating yourself. For example, I had to hold my 1-year old son for 14 hours during an international flight because he had a tough time falling asleep. Needless to say, I was on my feet for most of the time.

Recognition: talking about experiences that the listeners might have had in their past will cause a good laugh. Have you ever sung in a car by yourself without knowing the back windows were wide open? If the listeners had a similar experience, I bet that would cause a laugh. Now I know why people were looking at me.

Release: First try telling a longer story that creates tension, and then provide relief with a funny conclusion. My wife has a Crohn's Disease and a severe stomach ache occasionally. She went to an ER, thinking she might need surgery. The ER doctor told her she was pregnant.

A *day without laughter is a day wasted* – Charley Chaplin

77. Talk to Strangers

I mentioned how important it was to talk with strangers in a previous section (See the section: Network, Network, and Network). Let's cover the critical points in the art of talking to strangers.

Declare your interest by saying hi within the first 3 seconds: The first 3 seconds are the most important if you want to start a conversation. You can tell whether the other person is interested in a conversation based on their response. If you see someone you'd like to talk with and don't say hello within the first three seconds, you're likely to start overthinking and lose your nerve.

Tattoo their name onto your brain: Use whatever methods you need to remember their name at any cost. Remembering the name shows you respect the person. You can immediately control this conversation by calling their name frequently. Since I am a bilingual, I write the person's name on my palm in Japanese. The person has no idea what I'm writing, but I do it every time.

Have your set of 5 questions: Everyone hates the awkward silence... the longer it lasts, the harder it is to restart a conversation. We all have experienced that moment before, right? Your brain is working hard to remember the person's name, running at the max CPU rate. There is not much brain power left to do anything else.

How do you avoid that?

The answer is to have 5 simple questions on hand that you can ask anyone. You can expand the conversation based on the response. By having 5 simple questions already in your head in advance, you'll not have to use your brain power to come up with questions. Additionally, use the person's name as you ask each question. This improves rapport and helps you remember the name.

Find that person's Thing: No one hates to talk about their own interests or hobbies. I don't enjoy talking about my work but do enjoy talking about my hobbies. After saying hi, find out the thing which that person enjoys talking about. You can simply ask what their hobbies are, or what their passions are, which not only creates the rapport between you two but also makes the conversation with a stranger more enjoyable.

Give compliments: This never goes wrong. People like to hear compliments. Especially, if compliments are given to something the people care about.

Everybody likes a compliment – Abraham Lincoln

To be truthful, I still get a butterfly in the stomach when I initiate a conversation, but I enjoy the feeling. I'm more excited than nervous to get to know new people. Next time you fly or ride public transportation, give it a try. You never know what you'll discover unless you try.

78. Rock-Paper-Scissors: 100% Winning Strategy

How do you win in rock-paper-scissors every time? It's easy. Throw your hand after your opponent does. In other words, decide your hand based on your opponent's hand.

But that's cheating. Yes, you are right. You're not allowed to make your decision based on your opponent in the game of Rock-Paper-Scissors. But it is allowed in the game of communication. It's useful especially when you don't want to lose the game.

Let me give you an example. My wife wanted tiles on the kitchen floor but couldn't decide whether to go with a lighter or darker color. She asked me for an opinion. Here is some advice to any males reading this book. A question like that is a trap - it's a lose-lose option. No matter which you pick, you'll lose this game. After falling into similar traps and learning lessons many times previously, I knew what to do.

I didn't pick either.

Instead, I summarized what she had been saying about both options and asked her to focus on the pros rather than the cons of each color. Basically, I rephrased her words and shifted her attention to one thing (the pros). I didn't give my opinions at all.

Suddenly, it became easier for her to decide. After she chose the lighter color, I told her that was my preference, too.

I won the game by making my decision based on hers.

I felt great because it was beautifully executed. She must have felt great as well since she made the decision and I showed her my 100% support.

Wait, what if I really wanted the dark tiles? I would have emphasized the pros of the dark tiles more. That's all.

Opinion has caused more trouble on this little earth than plagues or earthquakes – Voltaire

I'm not suggesting that you not have your opinions. Everyone should have their own opinions based on their own beliefs. But it's always a good idea to know other people's opinions first if possible as it can save your relationships with them.

79. Body Language

Question: which part of your body gets enlarged when you see someone attractive?

I hope you don't have any dirty thoughts. The answer is your pupils.

Body language talks more than words. It affects how others see us as well as how we see others. Here is some body language vocabulary that gives cues to people.

Rapid Blinking: can be due to distress or discomfort
Lip Biting: can be due to anxiety and stress
Pursed lips: can be due to distrust or disapproval
Crossed arms: might indicate the person is defensive or closed-off
Standing with hands placed on the hips: might indicate the person is ready and in control (Power Pose)
Crossed legs: might indicate the person needs privacy
Tapping fingers and fidgeting: might indicate the person is bored
Closed posture: can indicate hostility, unfriendliness, and anxiety
Open posture: can indicate friendliness, openness, and willingness

Most importantly this non-verbal language can govern how we think and feel about ourselves.

Our bodies change our minds, and our minds change our behavior, and our behavior changes our outcomes.
— Amy Cuddy

What's powerful about body language is that you can control how you want to live your life. For example, before you go into a stressful situation like a job interview, do a power pose for 2 minutes. It's an indication of confidence and readiness. The power pose can increase your testosterone (yes, that's good for women as well as men!) and reduces the stress hormone called cortisol. Your performance will increase immediately. Most of the time, job interviews are not about the content of what you say, but rather are about the presence of how you look. (passionate, confident, authentic, comfortable, captivating, enthusiastic)

I personally visualize myself with a victory sign, and with arms up before I speak in front of people or even job interviews. That itself helps me calm down and puts me in a better mood.

CHAPTER 6: SELF-IMPROVEMENT

Here are random tips of self-improvements that I wish I have known earlier.

80. Stay Positive

During the recession back in 2010, I was fired from work. I had basically two options: to live my life holding a grudge against the company, or to move on with my life, thinking of it as a new opportunity. I personally know many people who have taken the first option. They don't look happy. With the second option, I was able to keep my head up, try different things, and land on a better opportunity. It's strange to say that I enjoyed getting fired.

There is nothing either good or bad but thinking makes it so. – William Shakespeare

In most cases, things will work out just fine eventually. Can you remember the last three things you worried about in the past and what the outcomes were? I bet most of you can't even remember what you worried about. Even if you remembered, I bet the outcomes turned out to be fine.

We humans are strong when it comes to adjusting the environment. My college coach says "S#!t happens; Move on". He is right. When it happens, we somehow overcome it or adjust to it.

James Lawrence, the Iron Cowboy, who completed 50 Ironman competitions on 50 consecutive days in 50 different states, fell asleep during biking and fell off the bike. His bike crashed, and he had a lot of nasty road rash. His feet were basically destroyed with blisters and his toenails were coming off. However, his body eventually adjusted to the environment 2 or 3 weeks into this event. Believe it or not, his time got faster and faster as the event went on. His fastest times were in the last 10 races.

Stop worrying about things, especially the ones you can't control, and cultivate a mindset based on optimism, positive expectation, and trust. I believe you'll be just fine.

81. Time Budgeting

No matter how much you wish for, you only get 24 hours in a day. Most of my days, 24 hours isn't enough. Some of you may feel that way, too. Having family makes me feel that way more than ever. I feel like the only way I have my own time is by sacrificing my sleep.

I ran into an article about Time budgeting. For Money Budgeting, you list your incomes and your expenses such as groceries, loans, entertainment, and savings. Ideally, your income shouldn't exceed your expenses including savings. Time budgeting is similar. You list activities such as work, sleep, relaxing, and so on. Again, the sum of the hours allocated into the activities should be equal to 24 hours. Once I finished my time budgeting, something seemed odd.

Activities	Hours
Sleep	6
Work	8
Lunch	1
Commute	1
Exercise	1
Family time	4
Total	21

I listed my daily activities and allocated hours. But it didn't sum up to 24 hours. Why? I don't do anything else major besides the items on the list. Where do the 3 hours go every day?

This was the first time I realized I had 3 hours every day for myself. Until then, I was always complaining that I never had my own free time to do whatever I wanted to do. Now I know I have 3 hours even after spending the four quality hours with my family.

Time Budgeting will allow you to make daily plans more effectively

Now that I know I have 3 hours, I use the time to recharge myself from work and family. We hear often that Life and Work balance is important, but we don't often hear that Alone time and Social time balance is just as important.

I don't get to spend my 3 hours of free time during the day though. It starts from either 5:00am or 11:00pm. Oh well, it's better than nothing.

82. How Should You Spend Time in Your 20s?

Your 20s could be your most defining decade. You'll have more freedoms, more choices, and more money (believe it or not) than you've ever had in the past or will ever have in the future. It's going to be a great adventure.

Here is a truth; how you spend your time in your 20s will define your future.

An advanced degree might be a great choice for you as your starting salary can be 20 (or more) percent higher than with a Bachelor's degree. I understand that you just got out of college and don't want to think about homework and exams for a while. The truth is continuous education is one of the keys to success in your life.

Traveling in the world and enjoying its many cultures will be another idea, as it might change your perspective on life. I highly recommend you travel alone as it forces you to step outside of your comfort zone and talk to strangers or the locals. Blake Mycoskie, the founder of Tom's shoes, got his idea of giving a pair of shoes when a customer buys a pair while he was traveling in Argentina. You never know what ideas and opportunities are lying on the ground during your travel.

Starting to manage your health by exercise and a proper diet will lead you to a better life in the future. By starting it in your early 20s, you'll establish a foundation for a healthy mind and body.

Pursue hobbies, start your own company, take high risks, jump on opportunities... there are too many possibilities to list here.

More demands professionally and personally will come later in your life. These things above will be much harder once you start a family. Imagine doing homework while your baby is crying in the background? How about kicking and screaming in the airplane on the way to your vacation? I've been there and done those. It wasn't pretty.

That being said, I can't emphasize enough how important it is to invest quality time with your friends. You don't have to have many. But you must have some. Quality is better than quantity.

Spend your time with one or two whom you can call best friends, who drop everything and come when you need them.

By the way, I'm not talking about your friends on social media. Meet and hang out with them. Go on road trips or backpacking in Asia together. You can only do so in your 20s.

The future depends on what you do today.
– Mahatma Gandhi

Time is the most precious resource that you have. Invest it while you have it.

83. Love Yourself

You should know you are beautiful just the way you are – Alessia Cara

No one will love you more than you'll love yourself. We all have certain things that we don't love about ourselves. But you have to love yourself in spite of those things. Love yourself even as you work on the parts that you don't love.

Hirotada Ototake was born in 1976 in Tokyo. He was a normal child except he was born without arms or legs. He overcame many heartbreaking obstacles and life ordeals throughout his childhood. Despite his disability, he sold over 6 million copies of his book, started multiple Non-Profit Organizations, and became one of the most influential people in the world. As a result of his self-love, he has accomplished more than ordinary people.

I totally understand that this is easy to say but hard to do. You might have gone through self-doubt and even self-loathing many times when you were a teenager. The truth is, whatever reasons you have for not loving yourself are all within your head. No one really cares about those reasons. Other people love you because of who you are, not what you are. So should you! Don't try to fit into social norms. Be who you are and proud of who you are.

You are unique, and that's your strength

Once you start accepting who you are and loving yourself, something remarkable will happen. It will give you the confidence to take the risks you need to, to keep going when you want to quit, and to believe in yourself to achieve something great. As I mentioned in the previous section, although I was fired from work, my self-love gave me the confidence to achieve something I'd never done before. Self-love is your first step toward your success.

If you are searching for that one person who will change your life, take a look in the mirror. - Anonymous

84. Unlock Black Boxes

Animals are fascinating to watch. They develop very unique skills and strategies to survive in the wild. Bottlenose Dolphins, for example, hunt with a group of 4 or 5 when they are in a shallow water. A pack leader swims toward a group of fish, making a circle around the fish and swiftly moving his tail along the sand to create a plume, which traps the fish in the circle. The fish have no other way to escape except in the air. The dolphins, then, open their mouths above the water and wait for the fish to jump into their mouths. The method is called Mud Ring Feeding. It's fascinating to watch.

Humpback whales hunt in the similar way except they use air bubbles to trap the fish. It's called Bubble-net Feeding.

Problem-solving is a key to survival. This applies not only to wild animals but to humans as well.

I'm going to provide you with a scenario and I want you to think about how you can unlock this black box for yourself.

Let's assume you are a real estate investor, who buys and sells houses (Flipping). You find an old vacant house in a great neighborhood. This house is indeed a rough diamond. You want to make contact with the owner and negotiate. The problem is you can't find the owner's name or address anywhere. This seems to be the reason why other real estate investors haven't bought this house yet.

What would you do? Take a minute or two to think

If you define the problem correctly, you almost have the solution - Steve Jobs

There are multiple actions you could take. Although we don't know whether your ideas actually would work, thinking about them is the important thing here. Ideas like this are unlimited. The more you think about them, the better you get. If you don't think about problem-solving daily, you might want to seek opportunities where you can constantly think about it.

This was an actual scenario that took place during the recovery from the recession in 2013. Here is what the real estate investor did.

He put a sigh on the front porch, which said "For Sale" with his phone number on it. People called the number, asking for the price. He said it was already sold. Eventually, the actual owner called him with anger. The owner either saw the sign or was told by his friends that the house was for sale. The investor explained his purpose and was able to purchase the house from the owner.

I don't think many people would come up with the idea of putting a "For Sale" sign in the front of someone else's house. In fact, you might've had a better idea. Who knows? Yet, all well-known companies have gone through or are going though countless problems and they are solving them. That's why they still survive.

In the next section, I'll give you more scenarios so that you can work on your problem-solving thinking.

85. Problem-Solving Scenarios

♦ Toilet bowl cleaning product

You are selling an Environmentally friendly toilet bowl cleaning product. You want to market it by showing that the product is non-toxic and safe. How would you do it?

Adam Lowry and Eric Ryan, co-founders of Method, took on the notion that "Green doesn't clean" by creating products that could clean without harming the environment. It was easy to show the product worked by making the toilet look shiny. However, it was not easy to prove the product was environmental friendly.

What they ended up doing was to **drink** the product. Yes, they drunk the Toilet Bowl Cleaning soap!! Their action immediately proved to the customers that they could trust the product.

Disclaimer: the company has been purchased since then. Please do not try to drink the product as they may be using different ingredients.

♦ Holiday Season Sale

Holiday seasons are the best opportunity to sell your product. You spend a lot of money on marketing, and people are now talking about it on social media. Next thing you know, the product won't be ready prior to the holiday season... What would you do?

This was exactly what Jen Rubio, CEO of Away, faced in her first year as the CEO. Away is a travel brand company that makes direct-to-consumer suitcases and other travel gadgets. What she ended up doing was to create a magazine and sell it for $250 with a coupon that could be exchanged for the suit case. Not only was the magazine a marketing tool, but also it kept the customers engaged and excited till the suit cases were available.

♦ Driving under the Influence

First, don't do it.

But what if you DO get pulled over and have to show your ID when you are under the influence of something? How can you reduce the chance of getting a DUI ticket?

Peter Griffin from Family Guy has an answer. He says "I got drunk and then got my picture taken. So that way when I get pulled over for drunk driving, I look the same as on my license."

I don't recommend driving under influence. But thinking outside box is the key here.

86. Note-taking

One way to implement problem-solving thinking in your daily life is to take notes. It's not just ordinary note-taking though. There is a good way.

I understand you've gone through college and thought you knew how to take notes. Well, so did I. This method allows you to summarize information, define problems and think about the solutions.

Here is how. On the left side in your notebook (first page), jot down whatever the information is given to you during a conversation or meeting. You use the one page writing the facts only. Divide the right side in your notebook into two sections, labeling them with "Problems" and "Solutions". See below

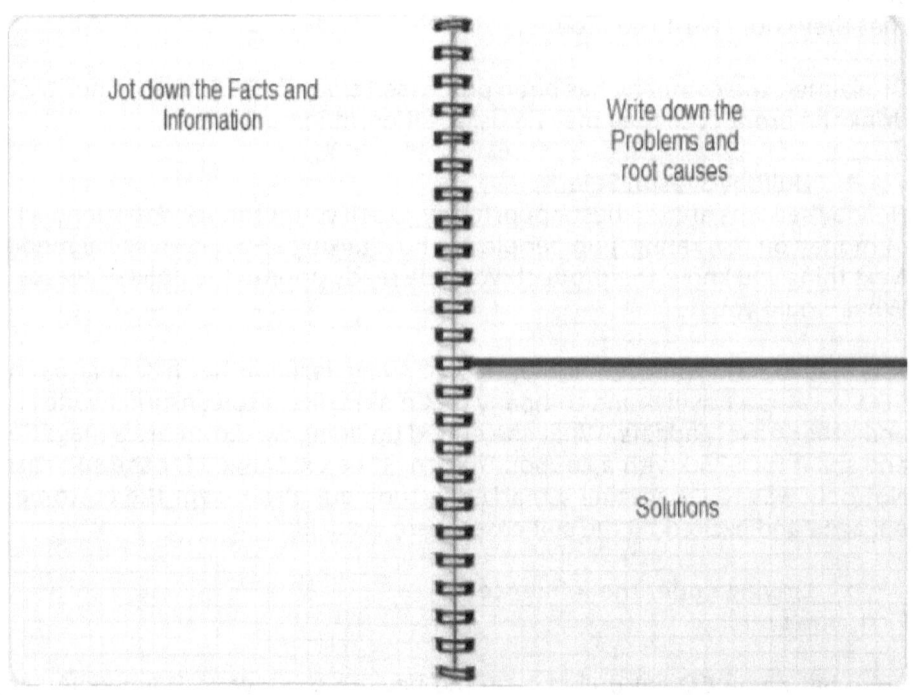

If I had an hour to solve a problem, I'd spend 55 minutes thinking about the problem and 5 minutes thinking about solutions – Albert Einstein

You should be spending most of your time in the problem and root cause section. You can even use the "5 Why" technique mentioned in the previous section to help you identify the issues.

One good thing is that you can do this almost anywhere. In a meeting,

seminars, group discussions, or even at a restaurant. When you find an issue in life, start a new page

87. Start Something

The best way to learn a new language is to live where the language is spoken. In other words, put yourself in a situation where you have to use it to survive.

The same concept can be applied to anything. If you want to become good at problem-solving skills, put yourself in a situation where you have to brainstorm and execute your plans to survive. The note-taking method in the previous section will help you develop the skill but that's like trying to learn a new language by writing and reading. It is important up to a certain point. But you'll truly learn the skill only by using it.

I recommend you start something new such as a meetup group, a Non-Profit Organization, a business... there are many options to start and follow your own passion.

You will learn what you don't know as you go, sometimes in a hard way.

This is the best time for you to learn as many life lessons as possible while taking risks. The sooner you learn, the easier things will get.

If I had to live my life again, I'd make the same mistakes, only sooner – Tallulah Bankhead

When you do start something, I want you to focus on Vision. Vision is the ability to think about or plan the future with imagination or wisdom. As I mentioned in the previous section, you get there much faster if you know where you want to go.

Vision without action is a daydream. Action without vision is a nightmare – Japanese Proverb

Although what you start may not last for a long time, the knowledge you'll acquire will be priceless and can be applied to future opportunities. Good luck!

88. To Be or Not to Be (Stressed)

What is your biggest stress cause? Work? Traffic? Bills to pay?

Stress is a burst of energy that basically advises you on what to do. However, when we hear the word "stress", we tend to associate it with a negative thing. Truth is that there is both good and bad stress.

Good stress, also known as eustress, is the type of stress when we feel vital and excited about life. You've felt it recently when you started a new job or undertook some project. It is very beneficial in our lives because it motivates us to achieve our goals and accomplish tasks. Researchers believe that it can help the immune system and protect our body from infection.

Bad stress, also known as chronic stress, is the type of stress we usually think of when we hear the word "stress". It is emotionally draining. It is harmful to our health and well-being.

Just like anything else, a little bit of stress is a good thing. Too much stress is a bad thing regardless of whether it's eustress or chronic stress. The key is how to manage and control the chronic stress in relationships. Here are 5 tips that can be easily done every day.

a) Breathe deeply and slowly: when stress hormones are released, you experience physical symptoms such as fast, erratic heartbeats and constricted blood vessels. Controlling your breathing can help activate your parasympathetic nervous system, which ultimately relaxes you.
b) Worry only about what you can control and accept what you can't. This is the mindset of "Go with the Flow". You shouldn't be upset about the traffic or weather. It is what it is. Crap happens. Move on!
c) Practice Daily Meditation: this is fantastic for maintaining your stress level, by joining your body and mind. One good thing is that you can do it anywhere, anytime. Try it first thing in the morning because it helps to set a calm tone throughout the day.
d) Light exercise such as yoga or walking: chronic stress in relationships, school, or jobs is mental. Putting physical stress on your body through exercise can relieve the mental stress. Even a quick 5-minute walk does the job.
e) Help others: a study in the American Journal of Public Health found that those who had gone through stressful events and then went on to help others had a reduced risk of stress-related mortality than those who didn't report helping others very much

Stress is not a bad thing.
Not being able to relieve stress is a bad thing.

There are many other ways to reduce stress other than the ones listed above. The bottom line is to maintain stress within a reasonable range. That is the most beneficial for our lives. Too little stress can cause lack of motivation to achieve our goals. Too much stress can be harmful to our health and well-being. Find what works the best for you and stick to it.

89. Friend or Foe

When I had just entered the real world, I read an article about friendship. That article has been stuck in my head since then. The article basically stated that we only need two best friends. The characteristics of best friends are

1. One with knowledge who knows what to do and can give advice
2. One with heart who drops everything and comes to you when needed
3. One with a smile who makes you laugh and is fun to be around

You become one of the persons based on your personality and find the other two.

I thought the article was interesting since I was looking for people with those characteristics after college. As you know, days are tougher, longer and more brutal in the real world than college. I needed someone like a mentor with knowledge who could assure me that I was on the right path. I needed someone kind who could help when needed. I needed someone funny who could make my day.

I had always been the kind of person who had a wide range of horizontal relationships but not vertical, meaning I had many good friends but no best friends. That was until the real world hit me in the face. I was desperate for best friends who had those characteristics.

One day I realized I always had those friends (that I call now best friends) around me. I saw it the whole time but just didn't recognize it. It felt like looking for a pair of sunglasses all over the house when they were on my head the whole time.

"Are we going to be friends forever?" Asked Piglet
"Even longer." Pooh answered

Since I started calling them best friends, our relationship became much better. Maybe that's why I see girls calling each other best friends (not so much among boys for some reason). Then I realized it was because of the power of labeling people. Let's talk about that in the next section.

90. Labeling Creates an Environment

Labeling people changes lives either positively or negatively, and it's very powerful. We need to use it with caution.

Here is an example, although my college degree wasn't Education, I taught in school right after college. Just like anything else, the more you do it, the better you get. Throughout my teaching journey, many mistakes led me to more effective and influential approaches to the students. This was experience and also conducting little social experiments with students.

One of my lessons I learned was to always label positively. When someone misbehaved and was labeled as a bad person, he ended up misbehaving again. When someone else misbehaved but was labeled as a good person in spite of their bad behavior, he ended up behaving better.

Why is labeling so effective? Because it's ultimately creating an environment where a person is continuously told that we do or do not believe in them, depending on their label.

If you want to change yourself, change the environment first

Have you ever seen a motivational speech or attended a seminar that got you excited? What happened once you got home? You probably lost the excitement, didn't you? it's like you are hot in the 90+ degrees outside, but once you go inside of a house with AC, your body is cooled down. If you want to stay hot, you need to stay outside.

Labeling has a similar effect by creating an environment. It can be used on yourself or others. For example, if you want to train for a 5k, label yourself as a member of a running club and join a team. Practicing with others as a member of a running club will help you achieve your goals.

91. Success

What is your definition of success and what are you doing daily to ensure that you progress towards that definition?

That is a good question to ask yourself occasionally to ensure you are walking in the right direction as the answer may vary throughout your life time.

Success doesn't come over night. It takes time and energy. As mentioned in the previous section, I highly recommend you design your routine for your success.

Humans are creatures of habit and routine. 95% unconscious and 5% conscious.

There are 6 steps to help you create a routine for success.

> 1. Link to the specific training mission: there is no need to reinvent the wheel if it already exists and has been proven to work. You just need a plan that you think will get you in the right direction.
>
> 2. Invest extraordinary energy for 90 days: It's not easy to commit for 3 months, but the hardest part is in the first few weeks. It gets easier as you continue. Persist!
>
> 3. Be precise in both timing and behavior: these will be the key to continue your journey.
>
> 4. Acquire only a few major routines at any one time: your brain and muscles work best if things are simple. Pick one routine to change at a time.
>
> 5. Focus on what you want, not on what you don't want: positive mentality works better in creating new routines.
>
> 6. Create a supportive environment: Join a club, make yourself be around people with the same goals, and keep each other accountable.

I define my success as living a happy and healthy life. The things I do to get there are simple things such as being in the moment, making time for social connections, taking stairs rather than elevators, and so on. Every time I add a new routine, I go through the steps to ensure the new routine will be done unconsciously.

Today, take time to ask yourself what the definition of your success is and what you are doing daily about it.

92. Leadership

Leadership is not for everyone, just like math (some people get chills even hearing the word "Math"). It comes to some more naturally than others. But either way it takes some time to master it. Even the most effective leaders had to practice a lot to get where they are now.

If you are interested in taking the role of leader one day, train as early as possible. As mentioned in the previous section, starting something new will put you in that role and give you opportunities to practice the skill.

What differences do you see between good and bad leaders? Good ones are nice, and Bad ones are jerks? Well, it's more than that.

Characteristics of Good leaders:
- Communicate effectively
- Lead by example
- Optimistic
- Open-Minded
- Demonstrate Integrity

Although the list is not exhaustive, Good leaders, without exception, have those characteristics, they excel at those skills.

Styles of Leadership:
- *Affiliative*: a leader who is collaborative and focuses on social and emotional bonds with others
- *Altruistic*: a leader who puts the others first and commits to build community
- *Authoritative*: a leader who is reliable and visionary
- *Bureaucratic*: a leader who likes discipline and enforces rules
- *Coaching*: a leader who helps individuals to achieve their full potential
- *Democratic*: a leader who collaborates and communicates with team members by providing opportunities for all to participate
- *Innovative*: a leader who is creative and helps others to see his vision of the future
- *Pace-setting*: a leader who focuses on productivity by setting high standards of performance

Understanding your leadership styles, which are based on your personal strengths and preferences, will help you become a more effective leader. Depending on your team or environment, you may have more than one style in order to lead different teams. This flexibility is a key to your success in any environment.

Reference: Understanding your Leadership Style from Toastmaster International

93. Decision-making

One true leadership skill is making decisions. Sometimes the decisions can impact many people's lives like nothing else. Leaders carry the weight of people on their shoulders.

It's scary. What if the decisions are wrong?

Leadership is not for everyone. Leaders have to have thick skins to make decisions which are not always right. But someone has to make them anyway.

This fear of decision making can be overcome. The following information will help you.

- **Not making a decision is also making a decision:** Remember that you learn something from mistakes. But you learn nothing from taking no action. In fact, indecisive leaders are worse than any amount of bad decisions.

- **You can't make everyone happy**: There is not a one-fits-all decision that we all can agree upon. You will hurt some people's feelings no matter what. Be proactive and reasonable with the decision, which should be based on facts, not your feelings. Be sure to back up your decisions through research and advice from knowledgeable people. Then the ones whose feelings are hurt will respect your decisions by communicating honestly.

- **You won't ever know all the information before you make decisions. No one does**: Studies found that fast decisions were far superior to slow ones. Information is always limited. You can certainly get more information by delaying the decisions. But that can be more damaging than anything else.

True leadership comes from the ability to make decisions even when you aren't sure if they are right – Tony Robbins

When it comes to decision making, be open-minded. No big decisions have to be made. Take baby-steps; test and learn from them. Decision making is a skill just like any other. The more you practice, the better you'll become.

94. Speak at a High Level of Consciousness

Let's name a few influential people. Jesus Christ, Augustus Caesar, George Washington, and Lady Gaga???

Have you ever wondered how they attracted and influenced people? It turns out they have one thing in common; they lived or are living at the highest level of Consciousness; Mission & Vision

There are 5 levels of purpose, or reasons for action. Let's go over using an example.

> 1. **Environment**: John works for a hospital because he lives nearby.
>
> 2. **Behavior**: John works for a hospital because he has experience in Physical Therapy
>
> 3. **Capability & Skills**: John works for a hospital because he has a degree in biology
>
> 4. **Value of work**: John works for a hospital because he believes he can fully serve the community by helping injured and sick people
>
> 5. **Mission & Vision**: John works for a hospital because he has a dream - One day he wants to find a cure for cancer

When you meet John and he tells you where he works and why, which John would you get impressed by? Most likely not #1, 2, or 3, right? They have a lower level of purpose. I doubt #1 John would ever impress girls at a bar.

#4 and #5 are very impressive, aren't they? Especially #5. Without exceptions, all the influential people are like the #5 John. They know their own destiny.

"Start with Why", by Simon Sinek, is a great guide for you to find what to do in your life. By asking yourself the right questions, you'll be able to narrow down the true path and see your destiny.

What is your life work? What do you want to accomplish? Where are you going with your life? With whom?

Make time to think of what contributions you intend to make to the world.

Sometimes you find it right away. Sometimes it comes later on in life. Things happen in life for reasons. The important thing is to know your destiny and be proud of it. Soon, you'll know that you'll influence others just like the people listed above.

95. Tips for Parents

My 9 years of teaching in high school taught me many valuable life lessons. I'm blessed to have had that opportunity prior to my first baby because I can apply some of that knowledge in raising kids. Or at least I thought I could. Little did I know that Parenting was another discipline I had to learn.

In this section, I'll share 3 valuable bits of information for parents. Regardless of whether you are already a parent or not, keep the information in your mind. You'll find it beneficial in raising your children one day. Remember that it takes a long time to teach kids good behaviors, but it takes even longer to unwind any bad information and reteach it again. Let's do it right in the first place.

- **Yelling is not communicating, as kids shut down instead of listening:**

I understand that you are stressed out from everything around you, including your significant other. You have very little room in your heart to allow misbehavior. When kids push a wrong button, it's easy to react with anger by yelling. Yes, I've been there.

Unfortunately, yelling won't get the kids' attention. Yelling will eventually become normalized, and the kids won't even listen. I don't blame the kids. In the end, who likes to get yelled at, right? Furthermore, the kids will yell too when they are in that situation, as they mirror the parents' behaviors. It'll be very difficult to discipline them in the future.

Speak quietly instead when the kids push a wrong button. They already know they are in trouble by the way you look. Calm them down first and set up an environment where they can hear you.

- **Strict parents will not raise well-behaved kids:**

Kids will behave well when they know WHY things should be done in certain ways not when the parents get mad.

For example, my kids fasten their own seat belts, because they know they will not see Dad and Mom ever again without it if an accident occurs. Now they check mine to make sure I have it on.

Explanation and redirection are much better options than telling them what to do or not to do.

- **Use the Magician's Select**

Have you seen a magic trick where a volunteer picks a card and the magician (magically) knows what it is? The trick is very simple - the magician controls which card gets picked. The audience thinks there are many options, but the outcome is always the same. That's called a magician's select.

You can apply the same concept on your kids. Communicate in a way that gives your kids a range of options but be sure that each option is one that you like. Your kid feels like they are holding all the cards. But they'll be playing right into your hands.

These skills require a lot of practices and patients. Enjoy the moment while you can!

96. Every Day Should Include a Nap

In the last 50+ years, sleep has been studied thoroughly to understand what it does to the body and how it impacts mental and physical health. One of the things they learned is that sleep is much more complicated than just dreaming.

The amount of sleep people need varies from person to person. In general, adults need from 6 ~ 8 hours a day.

A typical sleep cycle goes through the following stages:

> Non-REM 1: a transition period from being awake to falling asleep
> Non-REM 2: your breathing and heart rate will begin to slow
> Non-REM 3: a regenerative period where your body heals and repairs itself
> REM: your breathing and heart rate will increase and become irregular. We dream during this stage.

The cycle last about 90 minutes. During an eight-hour sleep period at night, a healthy person goes through the cycle 5 times. Ideally you want to wake up when a cycle ends (after 6 hours or 7.5 hours of sleep) to feel fresh in mind and body.

Why do we still get sleepy in the early afternoon after an amazing 8-hour of sleep? Can we blame it on the fries that come with a burger for lunch? The answer is deeply coded in our D.N.A.

Most mammals don't sleep for a long period every day because it increases the chance of getting eaten by their predators. Instead, they sleep for short periods throughout the day. Humans have changed the sleeping pattern to a longer period because we don't worry about the predators. The biological vestige, however, remains within us. Waves of intense drowsiness hit our bodies twice a day; in the early morning (from 2 am to 4 am) and afternoon (between 1 pm and 3 pm). Therefore, this early afternoon drowsiness is not a sign of laziness but a normal human behavior.

This midday wave of drowsiness causes diminishing of our reaction time, memory, coordination, mood, and alertness.

Reset your brain by taking a 10 ~ 20-minute nap

Scientific evidence shows that midday naps benefit both mental acuity and overall health. Napping, indeed, reduces stress and lowers the risk of heart attack, stroke, diabetes, and excessive weight gain. Some companies have adapted it into their cultures, having napping stations in the office.

The key is to sleep less than 20 minutes so that you stay in Non-Rem 1 and 2 stages. You'll feel sleepier if your nap is longer than 20 minutes as you enter into Non-Rem 3 stage.

97. Take a Detour in Your Life

Do you feel like you are sprinting in your life? You get out of high school when you are 18, out of college when you are 22, and now you are in the real world. You are doing the exact same thing millions of other people are doing or have done. I understand some did not go to college. My father didn't go to high school. My point is that you do not need to rush through your life. Taking a detour can do you more good than you think.

I sat next to a man named Ward on the way to San Francisco. He dropped out a college twice before he finally found what he wanted to do. In fact, he did so by accident. After he dropped out of his second college, he worked for a greenhouse company where their accountant had quit, but the position was never filled. He started organizing the files and realized that he enjoyed the work. He went back to a college a third time But this time, he knew exactly what he wanted to do.

From my personal experience, repeating my senior year in high school was the best decision I ever made. I decided to take a year off in my senior year and go to the US as an exchange student. Although I graduated from high school when I was 19 because of that, the year in the US changed the direction of my life by opening many windows of opportunity.

Now you are in your early 20s and excited about the real world. Your career is important, but that's only true if you find passion in your work. It's fine to take a detour to find what it is that you want to do in your life.

Taking a detour in your life might help you find your passion, as you get to experience new things through the journey.

You can do so in everyday life, too. Take a different path to work one day. It might be a faster than your normal way. You never know unless you try. You might find a nice coffee shop on the way or meet someone whom you wouldn't have met unless you took that detour. Opportunities are unlimited.

Sometimes it's the detours which turn out to be the fruitful ideas – Roger Penrose

Take a detour in your life and enjoy the view!

98. Want to vs Can

People quit jobs due to many reasons. One of them can be because the job is not something they want to do.

Ideally, you want to **figure out what you love to do, and then figure out how to get someone to pay you to do it**. If you find it meaningful and a purpose within itself, you are right where you want to be.

In reality, many people have jobs that are not what they want to do but what they can do.

Is that a bad thing? I believe it's not. Here are reasons.

- Increasing the number of your capabilities will open more doors for you

It's always nice to have many tools in your tool bag when you build a house. It'll be useful to have those skills when you finally get to do what you want to do

- What you want to do changes over time

What was your dream job when you were a little? Is it still the same? Probably not because what you want to do NOW might not have been an option when you were little. It might have changed many times as you grew older because what you wanted to do was replaced by outside information, unless it's coming from your heart.

Most Human desires are products of external environment and information.

- It gives a time to find what you really want to do

Those who know exactly what they want to do are blessed, aren't they?

Here is the downside. The longer you wait to start what you want to do, the harder it becomes to do. You'll pick up other responsibilities such as family, mortgage, loans, school, etc. I learned that the hard way.

Sometimes you find what you want to do accidentally. I didn't choose my first profession as a teacher. I happened to be at the right place at the right time to get the job. That was best thing that could have happened to me accidentally, and I'm grateful for that.

Keep your eyes, ears, and mind open. You might find opportunities everywhere.

99. Follow Your Passion While Living out Your Purpose

Passion: strong and barely controllable emotion. The origin is *pati*, meaning suffer in Latin.

The phrase "Follow your passion" is used by many motivational speakers. It's true that passion is what moves you forward and what helps you get back up when you fall. It is the fire within you.

The word, passion, comes from a Latin word Pati, which means suffering. There is definitely a connection between having passion about something and suffering. Despite the suffering, passion is worth having, and helps in achieving something great. In fact, it's necessary to be passionate about your dream to be successful.

But fire can't start itself, can it? It needs a medium such as wood or paper to keep the fire going. In other words, you need something else besides passion to keep going.

The medium or fuel in this case is "**Purpose**".

Purpose: the reason for which something is done or created or for which something exists

Purpose is the "Why" part of what you do. It's the core of your life work.

When things don't work out like you want them to, the fire within you can almost burn out. Yet, as long as you have the solid purpose within you, the fire will never burn out completely.

Following your passion without your purpose is dangerous. Know your purpose first before following your passion.

First find your medium, the purpose in your life. I know it's easier to say than to do. Keep open-minded and look for the clues. Sometimes people find theirs by accident.

Once you find your medium, your fuel, ignite the fire onto it. The clearer your purpose is, the stronger the fire will be and the easier for you to get back up when you fail. Oh, BTW, you will fail multiple times. Failure will be your best Sensei ever.

Next section will cover how people turn their failures into their assets.

100. Turn Your Worst Nightmare into Your Assets

Here is a question. Who failed the college entrance exams 3 times, got rejected from 30 different jobs and rejected from Harvard Business School 10 times? A hint: When KFC came to China, 24 people applied for the job. 23 of them got accepted, and he was the only guy who didn't. He also applied to a job in the Police force along with 4 other people. They got accepted, but not him. He also started his own ventures, then failed twice.

Yes, you guessed it right! It's Jack Ma Yun, the founder of Alibaba in China. He runs one of the biggest E-commerce networks in the world. Despite never having written a single line of code or selling anything to anyone, he turned his (many) failures into his assets and learned from them.

Many people who ended up with successful or meaningful careers, had hit rock bottom along the way to their success. To name a few -

Arianna Huffington, one of the world's 100 most influential people in Time Magazines, got rejected by 36 publishers when she wanted to publish her 2nd book.

Walt Disney was once fired from a newspaper because he was told he lacked creativity. His first animation company, Laugh-O-Graph, was forced to close, too.

Steve Jobs, the founder of Apple, was fired from his own company.

Milton Hershey, the founder of Hershey's chocolate company, started 3 companies that went bankrupt before his 4th company was successful.

The road to success is not easy to navigate, but with hard work, drive and passion, it's possible to achieve the American dream – Tommy Hilfiger

Learn from those failures. Continue learning throughout your career. If you think advanced education will be beneficial, then go back to school. It's never too late to learn. Leo Plass, the world's oldest college graduate, earned his degree at 99 years old.

101.   Sugar Lies

What do the Tobacco Institute and the Sugar Research Foundation have in common?

They both covered up lethal effects of the products they supported.

In 2016, researchers at the University of California in San Francisco revealed that an industry group called the Sugar Research Foundation quietly paid scientists to point blame at fat. The documents show that the foundation paid three Harvard scientists to publish a review of research on sugar, fat, and heart disease. In other words, the whole world was fooled by the foundation, believing that sugar was not bad for us!!

Henry Haas, the president of the foundation and an architect of this entire gimmick, knew that food makers would begin replacing fat with sugar once the research was published. He was right and made a fortune out of this incident.

That is not the only case. The New York Times revealed that Coca-Cola had provided millions of dollars to researchers to downplay the link between sugary drinks and obesity. It was Candy makers that funded studies of a claim that children who eat candy tend to weigh less that those who do not!

There are way too many processed, fructose rich, additive packed, and fiber-less foods out there, all of which contribute to obesity, and other health issues.

But that's not the only point I want to make in this section. What I really want to say is to validate or confirm any information you receive before you apply it to your life. You should even validate these 101 tips that are given to you in this book before you apply them.

No one is responsible for your life but you

Since it is hard to validate research results from Harvard University, we were all fooled by Henry Haas. It is a good idea to have a habit of challenging whatever information you see and understand the reason behind it. You'll have much less risk of going down a wrong path.

CONCLUSION

It's at 4:45am. This is the only time when the house is quiet so that I can write. In two hours, the kids will wake up and run around the house.

I've spent many days like this to write a few pages every day for the last one year. As I consider myself as a number person, writing is not my first nature. Plus, this is my second language. This experience has been more challenging than anything I've ever done before.

I was able to finish the book because I wanted to do one more thing for the former students of mine. I'm hoping they don't need any of my advice. If they do, I hope this book will help them move forward. I really wish them the best.

Although the majority of the readers are not my former students, I wish you the best, too.

Thank you for your time reading my book.

Regards,

Kaz Nagai

APPENDIX

Appendix 1: Loan Schedule

Loan Schedule	Mortgage Balance	No Emergency Fund
1	$157,592	$157,592
2	$155,063	$155,063
3	$152,408	$152,408
4	$149,620	$149,620
5	$146,693	$146,693
6	$143,619	$143,619
7	$140,392	$140,392
8	$137,004	$137,004
9	$133,446	$133,446
10	$129,710	$94,710
11	$125,787	$89,037
12	$121,668	$83,080
13	$117,343	$76,826
14	$112,802	$70,259
15	$108,034	$63,364
16	$103,027	$56,124
17	$97,770	$48,522
18	$92,251	$40,540
19	$86,455	$32,159
20	$80,370	$23,358
21	$73,980	$14,118
22	$67,271	$4,416
23	$60,226	-$5,772
24	$52,829	-$16,469
25	$45,062	-$27,700
26	$36,907	-$39,494
27	$28,344	-$51,876
28	$19,353	-$64,879
29	$9,913	-$78,531
30	$0	-$92,865

Note: At year 10, you pay off a portion of mortgage with $35,000 from your emergency fund. Open HELOC account in case of emergency.

ABOUT THE AUTHOR

KAZ NAGAI was born and raised in Matsue, Japan. He moved to US as an exchange student while he was in high school. He graduated from University of North Florida with a Bachelor of Science in Math in 2003, with a Master's degree in Secondary Education in 2005 and a Master's degree from Texas A&M in Statistics in 2017. He taught in high school and coached multiple sports, helping the young talent to achieve their highest potential. Although he eventually changed his career to be an actuary, his passion to help the young never died. He wrote this book primarily for his former students who were entering the real world, hoping this book would help them along their life journey.

www.ingramcontent.com/pod-product-compliance
Lightning Source LLC
Chambersburg PA
CBHW021145230426
43667CB00005B/261